WALKING on the CEILING

*The Practice of Overcoming Barriers and
Creating a Life of Freedom*

HEATHER MADDER

TATE PUBLISHING, LLC

Early Acclaim for *Walking on the Ceiling*

"Through her own experiences, Heather Madder teaches anyone who is carrying heavy burdens in life how to lift themselves through their ceilings of restraint and perceived limitations and actually "walk on their ceiling." A self-proclaimed "seeker of truth," Heather teaches us that the path to freedom involves a choice about where to stand, no matter what our circumstances, so that we can lift ourselves to higher heights. Gems of understanding which permeate the manuscript will lift your thoughts and help in your determination to be your own best!"

Linda Eyre, Co-Author of New York Times Bestseller *Teaching Your Children Values*

"Madder's Walking on the Ceiling is evidence that she has stared real life dead in the eye and come away a stronger, smarter, and better person for it. Her thoughtful and warm personal essays provide ample doses of hope and humor that will lift and entertain, and by the time they're done with her book, her readers will be convinced to "Bring what you have. It is enough.""

Chris Crowe
Author of the Award Winning *Mississippi Trial, 1955*

"You don't just read Heather's words, you savor the wisdom and truth on every page. An equally gifted speaker, her words stay with you long after you hear them."

Jannette Rallison
Author of *Fame, Glory, and Other Things On My To Do List*

"*Every ceiling when reached, becomes a floor upon which one walks on as a matter of course and prescriptive right.*"
~*Aldous Huxley*

Contents

Introduction

OF ALL THE HIGH STATIONS MANKIND CAN attain, freedom reigns supreme. When the bell of freedom rings out for nations in bondage, we rejoice as the people—the rightful owners of choice—recover what belongs to them. In the United States, we celebrate our liberty annually under a sea of fireworks that emit the glow of our great pride. We use the word "freedom" regularly in conversation and with such certainty that it seems we're convinced we possess it. However, even as we release the word into the air, we live captive under countless forms of bondage.

A myriad of invisible ceilings exist above us, and although we cannot always recognize them immediately, they leave evidence all around us. For example, most of us underestimate our worth as human beings as we wait for others to stamp us as "valid" because we cannot, or will not, do it for ourselves. Sometimes we are held captive by our own perceptions as we look at others, but never perceive who they really are. Though we may diligently post a flag to celebrate freedom, many of us remain emotionally imprisoned by the people we cannot forgive and past pain we cannot heal.

Specific ceilings hang over each of us, existing as a barrier that keeps us from the life that we want to have and the joy that we want to experience. They act as a boundary between who we are now and who we'd really like to be.

It is impossible to be human and not live under one type of ceiling or another. Yet there is a glorious truth that accompanies our condition. When we meet a limitation and expand beyond it, the boundary is absolved but we remain enlarged. For example, when we come to the ceiling of animosity and grow beyond it, the animosity dissolves, but an increase in character remains with us.

So it is with every other human limit we encounter. The same ceiling that holds us captive also has the power to exalt us. When we come to the edges of our borders and surpass them, we acquire the reward of expansion that lies within each one.

My first view of my own ceilings was an astounding one. Several years ago, many difficult circumstances coalesced in my life and knocked the wind out of the sails

For my Heavenly Father

I would like to graciously thank . . .

David, my husband, eternal partner, and closest friend. Words could never adequately express the breadth and depth of my love for you and my gratitude for the rich blessing of sharing our lives together.

My children, Jordan, Chase, Isaac, and Analiese who have filled my life with treasured purpose and infinite wonder. Also, my brothers, my sisters, and my mother for their great patience and love toward me.

My ANWA writer's group, Nancy Harline, Dave and Lois Madder, and many other friends and family members whose readings and encouragement of the manuscript brought me back to my desk time and again to continue the work. Also, Autumn McAlpin and Cherilyn Harline for their brilliant preliminary editing and valuable insights, and "Coach" Alison Jennings whose continual support and service has been a priceless gift.

The many students and fellow seekers whose letters, phone calls, and words of encouragement have blessed and fueled my writing and teaching over the years.

Most of all, my Father in Heaven and Savior, Jesus Christ, for their infinite endowments that I fully acknowledge I would be nothing without.

that had been transporting me along my path. These challenges awakened me to the reality of who I really was, and it was a stunning discovery. I was in bondage to my own thought patterns and chaotic emotional state. I was preoccupied by the physical world surrounding me, while the spiritual world was like a foreign land. And lastly, I was not fully present or authentic in my relationships with others. When you are only half a person, it is impossible for all of you to show up in relationships.

Change was an imminent reality, and I knew that I needed some solutions. In a menial attempt at improvement, I outlined a list of new goals that I believed would help me feel better about myself and my situation. I wrote out the list and put it on my dresser, and then I began to pray for help to achieve this new set of objectives.

Up until that time, God did not speak to me often—perhaps only a handful of times in my entire life. To me, He was like a cosmic bubble-gum machine in the sky. If I put in the correct coins and said the right things, I hoped that maybe He'd help me when I was really in a predicament. I didn't actually know Him. I wasn't totally convinced He knew me either.

However, on that particular morning, with the ink still wet on my new plan of attack, He spoke to my mind and gave me a message with unmistakable clarity. *You don't need a new list of goals. You need an entire transformation.*

No matter how deeply deception is imbedded

within us or how imprisoned we might be, when God speaks, His words cut through falsehood instantaneously, and the crimson truth spills out before us. Though I didn't know exactly what I needed, nor did I know how to find it, I believed that time and revelation would unfold the essentials to me. I tossed my small list of goals in the garbage and began a voracious search into the unknown.

That marked the formal beginning of my life as a seeker. Over the next few years, I worked diligently at discovering my boundaries and learning how to be free of them. I spent a great deal of time in solitude where I'd reflect quietly and seek God in meditation and prayer. As a genuine relationship slowly emerged with my Eternal Father, sincere and heartfelt prayer became an indispensable lifeline to my journey.

I began to seek as much knowledge as possible, reading early in the morning and late into the night. I listened to books on tape while driving in the car, and set up makeshift book holders so I could read while doing the dishes. To this day, the pages still carry water-worn imprints.

I also began to explore the back roads of my existence through writing. One reeling sentence at a time, I filled hundreds of pages of notebooks with thoughts and insights. I became the great observer, like a scientist watching an experiment. Life was my field study, but I had no hypothesis, just one driving quest for freedom. As the search commenced, I felt that my mind needed answers like my lungs needed air. Slowly, one deep breath at a time, the shackles began to slip off of my wrists.

It is now many years later, and though I still have much traveling to do, time and revelation kept their early promises. When I think back on the person I used to be, I feel as though I am talking about someone other than myself. Yet instead of distaste, I feel compassion for her. She represents a collection of experience, the hope of transformation, and the miracle of healing.

Today my mission of seeking truth still burns a path within me, but it is also blazing a trail that now leads beyond me. I have spent the last several years teaching others about spirituality and freedom. Whether in public circles or private tables, the process has emerged into this written compilation of essays, which address common boundaries that so many of us experience. They present a small sampling of ways to create a life that is founded in personal freedom and for which joy is a regular occurrence.

However, I am cautious in this venture. Truth exists in the universe independently of all of us. Yet it only enters the world through us, no matter how inadequate we may be. On the very best day, human instruments are still faulty vessels. The only answer to this predicament is to ask the reader not to look *at* the writer, but *beyond* her—further than the faulty instrument and become connected to God, the Divine Source from which all truth descends. Then we are both free, the reader and the writer, to transform and progress as God dictates individually to each of us.

In accordance with the natural flow of human development, we do not learn all the things we wish to in one great sweep of enlightenment. Ounce by ounce, we soak up and squeeze out insight from the sponges of truth. As we travel, we store in the buckets of our soul what we have found, and it evolves us. Then one day we look up where the ceiling used to be and realize that it is now beneath our feet.

Part 1

Freedom Within Us

1

Keys of Wholeness

Insecurity

I WROTE SWIFTLY IN THE THIRD BATHROOM stall at the Olive Garden, scratching notes on a blue spiral notebook I had grabbed from home on my way out the door. My husband and I had just enjoyed a quiet dinner together, and as he waited for the bill, I stole minutes from the evening to scribble a few of the words that swirled in my head and begged for release.

Many of my essays begin, as this one did, in the most unusual places. While my fellow female occupants in the restroom contended over which color of lipstick to apply and readjusted the straps of their dresses, I huddled fully clothed on the other side of the locked door with a pen in hand.

I began writing five years ago when we were transplanted from a small city in Idaho to Pittsburgh, Pennsylvania. Collectively, we were a family unit, but individually, everyone seemed content but me. I was a small person absorbed by a big city, and I felt that I had no real place—there or anywhere. In the mirror, I saw "David's wife" and "Jordan's mother," but once again, *I* had again failed to fully arrive with us.

Confused and empty but looking for fulfillment, I threw myself into as many passions as I could access. I searched for completion in friendships, shopping, a career, physical fitness, and a variety of pastimes. I felt that if I could somehow add more to myself, then there would finally be enough of me to feel good about.

After trying and failing and trying and failing some more, I finally realized that no magical solution was going to make me whole. A successful job wouldn't truly fill me. A perfect body wouldn't create the sense of completion I craved. More outer success couldn't make more of *me*. Each of these would, at best, divert my attention from my core problem, but there was no outside source that could truly complete me. I was the only one who could do so, but sadly, I was not yet present in my own life.

I had hit my head against the ceiling of my insecurities for so many years that finally, skull throbbing,

I had reached my level of tolerance for pain. At that point, I was willing to seek for wholeness no matter the cost of time or effort it required.

The first thing I did was pray to God and diligently and sincerely ask for help on this personal quest. I didn't know the way, but I believed that He did. Then I began to ask questions. I sent deep and probing queries into the darkness of the unknown with a modicum of faith that answers would return to me. Why did I feel incomplete? What was the origin of my many fears? How could I—a person who had felt inadequate for so long— finally experience wholeness?

I committed myself to an inward search every evening. While our boys were in bed, my hands wrote hour after hour after hour, exploring the crevices within me. That time became the most sacrosanct part of the day. While the washing machine rested and the dishes dried by air, I embarked on a more important kind of housecleaning.

Like an inquisitive child, I grabbed whole sections of my life by the fistful and dissected my inner world as the tip of my pen met the top of a blank sheet of paper. As dusk approached, I opened the window shades to let in the last few rays of the sun that sank into the western sky. Night after night, it descended and promised to rise again in the morning. Night after night, I wrote, hoping that a whole person might also arise with the coming day.

In time, my Eternal Father received my small crumbs of faith and returned my questions with tiny morsels of insight each day. He taught me that I looked for security from anywhere in the world, but never from myself or from Him. I realized that I sought for approval and fulfillment from ephemeral sources that could only inflate my ego, yet never truly fill me. If I was perceived in a positive manner by those around me, I felt valid. If I did "important" things, I felt worthwhile. However, if outside sources could give me the approval I needed, they could also take it away. Therefore, my flawed sense of completion rested on ever-shifting fault lines.

These initial inquiries and the answers that followed were keys that unlocked a floodgate of understanding, a grand comprehension that eventually unfolded before me. This process also birthed an authentic relationship between my Eternal Father and me in which I came to know that He is the source of all truth. As such, He is also the source of freedom. He is a generous Giver to those who search for Him, and He delights to heal His children who are broken and bound by falsehoods. If we become seekers, He is the one who teaches us to part our ceilings and travel beyond them in freedom.

There is a natural law that states that creators produce offspring like themselves. A lion produces a young lion, an oak tree produces a young oak tree, and even a blade of grass will bring forth a creation like unto itself. How odd would it be to find that your cat had given birth to a litter of parakeets or that the family dog had produced six young boa constrictors? This law is so common in our world that we would never consider it to be otherwise. Creators produce offspring like themselves. If this law exists in our physical world of creation, how could it not exist—even more perfectly—in the spirit world of creation?

Our Eternal Creator is a Being of perfect worth who is peaceful, loving, and intelligent. When He created each spirit, He transferred these traits to us. Though these qualities are young and not fully developed, at our spirit center we share similarities with the One who made us. We naturally inherited peace, love, wisdom, and most certainly—absolute worth.

That is not the truth we are taught in the physical world. Even though we were created by God, we now live among human beings, and the human world is immersed in scarcity. Here we are taught that high value is limited; therefore, we must compete for our portion. We are taught that love is in short supply, and so we must earn it. We are taught that confidence and security are only for those who prove themselves worthy. Thus insecurity is behavior we have learned. When we were born, we loved ourselves, but as we grew, the world taught us not to. As young children, we were secure, but eventually, we succumbed to beliefs of inadequacy.

Unfortunately, a system of scarcity is imbedded within our very culture. Those who have "more"—more money, more beauty, or more talent appear to be exalted in worth. Those who have "less" feel the pain of an apparent decrease in value. Of course, the entire system is incorrect, but that doesn't prevent the world from paying homage to it. These falsehoods are not only perpetuated in our culture, but parents can easily project their own feelings of scarcity onto their children. Without examination and cleansing, a new generation is then born and bred under the ceiling of insecurity.

The theories of the world are not our only hindrances. When our eternal spirits partnered with a human body, we inherited a physical packaging. Within that packaging exists what has been called the ego, the flesh, the natural self, or the carnal presence. The carnal presence is a feeling within, often manifesting as a voice in our heads, which constantly asks the question "Am I enough?"

This presence generates continual thoughts of inadequacy, which easily form an entire paradigm of insecurity. When we believe the thoughts and take them for truth, they produce fearful emotions within us. Together, the thoughts and the fears yield a false, but very influential reality—that we are inadequate beings. If we don't know otherwise, that false reality becomes our *only* reality. It causes us to feel insecure about our worth and propels us to struggle to obtain the value we already possess.

Insecurity operates as an internal vacuum that seeks to fill itself. Like all vacuums, it sucks. Insecurity sucks in praise from others and prompts us to prove ourselves to the people around us. We become intently concerned about how we are being perceived, and we seek to drop or manipulate information in a way that we feel will impress others. Some attempt to mask their insecurity by exerting bold confidence, yet fear may be the wind that blows behind their social sails.

Intimate relationships are another place where inward lack seeks fulfillment. We feel that if we could just obtain that one special relationship, then we'd finally feel whole. Unfortunately, the vacuum of insecurity usually sucks the life out of the loving relationships we do have. It dictates that even if we're loved, the love doesn't feel like enough. Even if we're praised, the satisfaction fades and leaves us looking for more. Blind to the truth, we often blame other people for the fact that we don't feel whole, secure, and at peace with ourselves.

Without spiritual wholeness, we easily become obsessed with temporal representations of value such as our physical appearance, making money, acquiring new possessions, or gaining power. We feel certain that these things will bring the satisfaction we seek. This causes us to become consumed by the future, because we believe that through some future achievement, we will finally be declared "enough." Of course, by themselves, achievements and possessions are not necessarily harmful. However, when the carnal presence attaches a self-inflating agenda to them, they become part of a damaging mirage.

The carnal presence has base instincts, and by nature, it can only serve itself. It is terrified to surrender its ulterior motives with the physical world and behaves as an enemy to our spiritual wholeness. Even if it harms our relationships, our finances, our health, or our well being, it will seek solely to fulfill its unending desires. The only point at which it feels satisfied is in the brief period of elation that occurs just after acquiring what it seeks. Yet soon the emptiness returns. Because the carnal self arises out of insufficiency and seeks hollow sources for fulfillment, it has no potential to transcend its own scarcity.

While the carnal presence tells us to keep searching in the world for our security and identity, the Spirit tells us that this world cannot grant either. It never has, nor can it possibly do so in the future.

The only power that can absolve the human inadequacy from which we suffer is the power of God. When we become wholly connected to our Eternal Father, our relationship with Him causes us to feel certain that we are literally His creations, and as such, we inherited worth that cannot be changed or destroyed. Paul teaches, "The Spirit itself beareth witness with our spirit, that we are the children of God" (Romans 8:16). When all of who we are becomes immersed in the reality of our spiritual identity, we wrestle ourselves free from the insatiable need to search for our identity in the world.

When God declared his existence to Moses he said, "I am that I am" (Exodus 3:14). He did not make a list of His qualifications, possessions, talents, or works of wonder to describe Himself. Though His works are astounding and magnificent, He merely said "I am." However, when we make statements of our existence, we usually skip over "I am," because we are so attached to what comes after it for an identity. "I am *affluent.*" "I am *educated.*" "I am *overweight.*" "I am *divorced.*" "I am *unqualified.*" We do not often feel that just to be—*just to exist*—is a valid reason to possess absolute worth.

When we live from "I am," our identity is rooted in its indestructible core. This allows us to abandon our agenda with the physical world. We may still participate in this world, but we no longer seek to find ourselves in any facet of our temporal existence. We are not our careers, our education, our possessions, nor are we the numbers on the bathroom scale. We are not our accomplishments or failures, the people who have raised us, or even the traumatic circumstances of our past. These things can be added to or taken away from our outer life, but our divine identity operates in its own eternal dimension.

Of course, we will never truly be free from the condition of human insecurity until we actually *experience* our spiritual identity. Spiritual truth comes through spiritual channels. We access these channels by immersing ourselves in God's teachings and by using His designated line of communication, which is prayer. We must spend time in purposeful meditation, reflection, and peaceful solitude, preparing to receive the full truth of ourselves and our lives.

Today I seek periods of stillness in which I reconnect to my own spirit. I sit quietly and feel the vibrant force of spirit life that is wearing this body and giving it breath. This, *I know*, is who I really am. I pray for an increased ability to abandon the thought patterns and the emotions of scarcity. I ask Him to teach me His eternal truths and grant me the power to build my life upon the principles of freedom.

Like a young pianist, we must always fine-tune the instrument of our own wholeness. We must return to the forgotten piano in the attic, wipe off the dust, sit up straight, and fumble our fingers around on the keys. We play poorly until we learn to play better; we stumble with the truth of what we're learning, until we find a place of permanent footing.

Fortunately, He promises, "For every one that asketh receiveth; and he that seeketh findeth; and to him that knocketh it shall be opened" (Matthew 7:8). Many of us have already spent a lifetime pursuing a physical mirage and have, at best, achieved momentary satisfaction. Therefore, the effort required to seek our divine identity will always be so little compared to the

permanent freedom and peace this discovery will distill
into our lives.

Today the sun rose in full radiance, bringing the
bursting light of day with its warmth. The morning came,
just as promised, and all of me rose with it.

I am at home finishing the essay that I started in
the bathroom of the Olive Garden as the words continue
to fill my head, waiting to find their place on a page. The
words don't question my fumbling abilities, and I have
learned not to question what they are teaching me to say.
They are wiser than I am.

At times, my vacuum from the past awakens.
When I first began to compile my essays into a book that
I hoped to publish, fear roared aloud in my head, cap-
tured my attention, and stifled my work. *You will never
be good enough to do this. You will only fail if you try.* One
evening, as I fell asleep, in that moment when the conscious becomes hazy and the unconscious becomes clear,
the voice of truth spoke to me again saying, "Bring what
you have. It is enough."

The carnal self may always ask the question, "Am
I enough?" But only through God, will we come to the
answer.

I am.

2

The Stillness

Chaos

THERE IS A TANGIBLE SILENCE IN THE woods, when the thickness of absence becomes perceptible. The stillness that surrounds me is a solid, comforting presence on this particular Thursday afternoon as I bike along wooded trails among circling hills. I appear to be alone, but my deeper senses know better.

Life surrounds me. An entire living world is balanced by intricate delicacy, one organism feeding on the decay of another, and the whole of it surviving in the process. God knows how to use what is discarded to keep His creations thriving, and mankind would do well to follow Him.

Slender, staff-like blades of wild grass separate to allow the passage of a small creature bearing a lavish, chestnut-colored tail. Then they close again to conceal their secret. A wood thrush dances in a canopy of hemlock, beechwood, and maple trees that obstruct the sun and offer me a thick, peaceful shade. Sinuous hillsides flaunt billowing mounds of greenery, like overflowing baskets of cotton. I love the trees and they love me back. They are more than foliage—they are great figures of rescue.

The trees of Frick Park carry secrets they will not disclose. They hold the heat of a thousand runners. They carry the salty drops of bikers' ambitions. They hide hundreds of first kisses and pints of blood etched by thorn-clad branches that refuse to bend for a hiker's passing. Iron Gate Trail holds mounds of my thoughts, but the eastern hemlocks promised not to reveal them.

Eyes open wide, I ride along. A monarch butterfly alights on an upturned leaf and then gracefully flies away. A spider inches its gangly legs along the perimeter of my path. I ride on a man-made trail, but it's clear that I'm a visitor here, and the creatures to which this place really belongs decidedly ignore me. We share the same space, and I promise to honor their world in exchange for a late afternoon passing.

One might be surprised to find that these lush, silent woods stand directly in the middle of the flourishing city of Pittsburgh, Pennsylvania. It is no small miracle that 250 acres of densely wooded terrain remain untouched by the ambitions of industry that cleared so much of the surrounding land for monetary purposes. A few miles in any direction would place me directly amongst six lanes of speeding traffic, towering buildings, and garbage-lined streets. Discovering these woods was more than exciting; it was like stumbling upon a diamond in a dark and yawning cavern.

In 1908, an industrial millionaire asked his daughter what she wanted for her debutante party on her seventeenth birthday. She asked for a place where children of the city could enjoy nature.

He said yes.

Nearly one hundred years later, these sacred acres are a place for us to come back to God after we've been to work and to the bank, and to come back to ourselves after the calendar has abused us. I'll always revere Helen Frick for asking her father to safeguard this land in a way that would best preserve the souls of its inhabitants.

My legs blaze with pain from the uphill climbs, but adrenaline soothes their ache as I barrel back down the narrow passages. I love this bike just less than my children. Frick Park is my sacrosanct haven and a sweet release from the life that runs me over. I leave my watch in the car so that I will not taint the day with the hands of a time god that usually holds me captive. However, it's the silence that I come for, the viable force that heals my humanity and remains with me when I resurface from this richly wooded haven.

As the sun sinks slowly behind the lapping leaves and the light retreats to its own celestial refuge, I know I must leave as well. The only thing I take with me from the woods is the stillness.

A grave ceiling that hangs over our planet is the lack of connection we have with the world beyond this one. Noise and confusion congest the lines of communication that must remain clear in order for us to tap into the spiritual realm of God. That realm is best accessed through stillness.

Stillness is a living current of peace that pulses through the universe, and when we immerse ourselves into its stream, it flows through us, connecting us to God. It is in this dimension of divinity that we saturate our lives in the intangible, yet essential matters of the soul.

Eckhart Tolle teaches that stillness is a part of our innermost being, and "when you lose touch with inner stillness, you lose touch with yourself. When you lose touch with yourself, you lose yourself in the world."[1] When we are disconnected from God and His spirit, the truth of who we really are and our higher purpose for living are lost to us.

Every person in the world can find stillness, even if his or her life is very busy. In the morning, I take a few moments, close my eyes, breathe deeply, and focus on the spirit life that is inside of me. It's a simple gesture, but it reminds me that while my outward life is tied to the world that I can see and touch; my inward life has forged a bond with its Creator. A unique form of prayer, my small, human soul reaches out to the great and powerful God, beyond itself.

In these moments, peace begins to vibrate gently through me, and I take it with me when I wake my children, when I discuss finances with my husband, or when I walk out the door into the world. Even if my schedule is outwardly hectic, there is stillness within. Kahlil Gibran observed:

> There is something greater and purer than what the mouth utters. Silence illuminates our souls, whispers to our hearts, and brings them together. Silence separates us from ourselves, makes us sail the firmament of spirit and brings us closer to Heaven; it makes us feel that bodies are no more than prisons and that this world is only a place of exile.[2]

Periods of silence, large or small, do indeed cause a separation to occur. They edge a space between the tangible, physical part of our existence and the deep, abiding presence of our inner spirit life. Stillness allows us to connect with the latter of these two and tap into our spiritual homing device—the deepest part of us that instinctively knows that our real home is not this earth. A life without stillness is a life disconnected from the very real divine current trickling through this physical world and calling us to seek the next one.

Our Creator has spoken, "Be still and know that I am God" (Psalms 46:10). Be *still* and *know*. Stillness is the partner of knowing, because in the quiet veins of stillness, we reach the deepest dimension of knowing. It is quiet, but sure; it is still, but certain. After periods of silence, we exist in a state of being that is more divine than just being human. Our lives reflect a meaning, a knowing, that did not previously accompany us.

We live in a world of prolific information, where facts are bought and sold in countless institutions. However, our world does not need more information to catalog and memorize as much as it needs more truth and wisdom to live by.

Essential knowledge cannot be bought or sold. It is only through divine channels that this information becomes embedded into the human soul. For example, as a young woman I had been taught about someone called God. Though I knew many facts about Him, it was through stillness that I experienced my Creator as a loving Being who was intimately connected to my life. That is when knowledge became more than mere facts. It was alive within me.

Later it was through stillness that I understood that responding to people with love would ease much of the unhappiness that I experienced in my relationships. Though I mentally believed in the concept of love, this principle sprouted to life within me when it was fed by the deeper venues of spiritual intelligence.

As transforming creatures, we are prone to publicize our new goals of change. Yet when stillness teaches us, the fruits are not loud, temporary whims that we scrawl onto 3 x 5 cards and tape to our bathroom mirror. The quiet nature of the knowledge lends itself to steady, private change as we purposefully move in a sound direction.

Unfortunately, silence is becoming scarce among us. Noise has become a ceiling that we live beneath that blocks our access to the stillness of God as well as to deeper truths. The constant flow of television, computer, and audio stimulation offers a cheap substitution for authentic living. It inhibits us from experiencing entire sections of our lives in the depth that they require. Instead of mending an unraveling relationship, we log on to the Internet. Instead of addressing our pain, we turn up the volume. Instead of reaching toward God, we reach for fictitious drama in vivid color.

A life too full of audio-visual stimulation is a surrogate life for those who ought to be experiencing their own. Media can be a delicious, but hazardous pastime, one for which we will pay dearly as meaningful segments of our lives are drowned out by the noises that we invented and continue to invite.

Some claim to feel bored when they are surrounded by silence. However, stillness is the space where we meet ourselves and where God comes to join us, if invited. The pristine reality of our lives is revealed to us and future paths become clear. What could be more interesting? When we feel that we have nothing outwardly to do, we know that inwardly, there is much to do.

The tranquil rivers of truth invite us to their waters, but their wisdom cannot be transferred through the superficial layers of existence. Our entrance is delayed by distractions from a modern world, which is both blessed and hindered by its own progression. We must ask ourselves if progress has really furthered mankind. In our mad pursuit of acquiring, have we secured anything long lasting like greater peace, increased love, or deeper wisdom? Modern technology offers immeasurable conveniences, but we can easily become focused on quantity of consumption rather than true quality of living.

Authentic quality of life cannot come from the physical world. It is a richness found only by living in union with our Creator and in harmony with his eternal truths. Stillness is the door we enter that allows us to spend time with God, and when daily life dictates that we must leave, it is *Him* that we will take with us.

3

Awakening

Unawareness

I HAPPENED TO GROW *TOGETHER* IN A café. Though I grew *up* under the watchful care of my parents, I didn't assemble the pieces of myself as I ran through the sprinklers and wrapped my lips around root beer popsicles. Growing older never really ensured that I was growing whole as a human being.

Looking back, adolescence was a rocky road of acne and insecurity, and as I became a teenager, I was well intended, but scattered. When I first left home as an "adult," the college experience didn't bring me to completion either. The agenda of my coed existence was to ingest information, regurgitate it with a #2 lead pencil, eat microwave burritos three times a day, and date ambitious, young males in my spare time. Surprisingly, spiritual wholeness didn't find me during that schedule.

It took twenty-five years of dense living before I paused long enough to process the minutes, hours, and days of my existence on this planet. Ironically, two helpful aids in growing together as a person were a notebook and a quiet place—a café, a desk at the library, or even a park bench. It's noteworthy that reflective solitude did more for my transformation in a matter of months than did my entire career of rigorous academia.

Visiting a coffee shop is unusual for a woman with a health commitment that doesn't include coffee. Yet I didn't go for the beverages; I went for life. I went for a place to write fragmented sentences about a fragmented person and to work at bringing them both to completion.

Though hot drinks wake millions of minds in the morning, it is alert attention that awakens people to the awareness of their own existence. Jon Kabat-Zin calls this "mindfulness" and teaches that it is "the art of conscious living." In *Wherever You Go, There You Are* he states:

> *Mindfulness means paying attention in a particular way: on purpose, in the present moment, and nonjudgmentally. This kind of attention nurtures greater awareness, clarity, and acceptance of present-moment reality. It wakes us up to the fact that our lives unfold only in moments. If we are not fully present for many of those moments, we may not only miss what*

is most valuable in our lives but also fail to realize the richness and the depth of our possibilities for growth and transformation.[3]

Mindfulness is a tool that helps us dispel the fog that impedes our ability to see ourselves, our own minds, and the intricate segments of our lives clearly. Without the lucidity that comes from the "present moment reality," many things close to us can fall apart beyond our view: the relationship unravels, the finances spin out of control, our health diminishes, or the child turns away from us. It is impossible to navigate our lives well if we cannot see what is in front of us. Awareness is the sharp ray of clarity that cuts through the dense mists of denial and self-deception. It prompts us to examine our inner state and interrogate it in detail:

"Why am I tense?"

"What is this pain?"

"Why am I afraid?"

When we ask open-ended questions, our eyelids raise. When we pay attention, our vision widens, and when we finally understand the answers, they liberate us.

At Walden Pond, his own place of solitude, Henry David Thoreau observed, "Only that day dawns to which we are awake."[4] Just because we get out of bed every day doesn't mean that we're really awake in our lives. For us to be fully awake, we must be fully *aware*.

Unfortunately, we've been programmed for pro-duction. We've been taught to put a smile on our face and keep it together, even if all the pieces inside us have toppled over. However, mindfulness teaches us to tell the truth about our condition—if not to the world, at least to ourselves. Of course, it takes great courage to see the whole truth of our lives. Often we're afraid to see ourselves the way we really are for fear of what we'll find. Even worse, we fear that if the truth is revealed to others, they won't accept us, and acceptance is what we desperately crave. It takes persistent bravery to seek the truth and to stay with it long enough to heal our broken places. Unfortunately, many refuse to pay close attention to their inner selves. They choose, by default, to submit to a life of bondage rather than execute the search for their freedom.

Along with meditation and observation, writing can be a very effective tool that aids the process of aware-ness. Sometimes a fast-flowing pen and a well-filled note-book can be instrumental in introducing people to their own lives. In *The Right to Write*, Julia Cameron states,

> It is human nature to write. We should write because humans are spiritual beings, and writing is a powerful form of prayer and meditation, connecting us both to our own insights and to a higher and deeper level of inner guidance. We should write because writing brings **clarity** and passion to the act of living.[5] (Emphasis added by this author).

My own writing life was birthed out of a need for

survival. I was in bondage and in great pain because of it. A desire to ascend that pain planted seeds of introspection, and in time, those seeds sprouted into a written path of higher wisdom. I wrote about everything—my past, my fears, my relationships, my future—with the intent to understand. When I wrote soulful questions on a page, a Divine Force returned the answers. My eyes opened inward, and as the lines on the page began to fill, I started to see myself and my world clearly for the first time.

Writing is a tool that allows me to shove my knuckles into the middle of my gut and pull out the honest core. When my hand flows loosely across the page, the words may be illegible, but inner truth becomes crystal clear. It is when my fears fade into the floor, and I begin to stand up straight again. It is when an old upset turns to compassion, now that I understand all the pieces. And when my prayers rebound from my bedroom ceiling, writing becomes a personal form of prayer that allows me to reach out and put my own hand into the hand of God.

My old notebooks have become personal maps. Crude records of my evolution as a human being, they are the places I've been and the places I hope never to be again, and I keep a fresh one within arm's reach for any new awakening to be recorded. They are by my bed, in my purse, next to the couch, and in the car. They only cost me 89 cents, but they carry more value than all the material things I own times twelve.

On the outside of the windowpane of the corner café, crowds of people bustle unconsciously along the sidewalks of life. Yet inside, a select few so richly cherish it. On a terra-cotta couch with notebooks in our laps, we take pause to say to the universe, "I'm right here."

We stand in direct rebellion to the gas station diet of existence. Behind these doors, life isn't served supersized in a Styrofoam cup with a straw to increase inhalation capacity. Instead, it is steamed, frothed, and stirred in crafted pottery that's been shared by a few hundred patrons. On seasoned corners, perhaps a thousand have sipped from one rim. We don't gulp down our existence while speeding on an austere highway to the accompaniment of a Chevrolet horn. We savor it while violin music unravels a melody in the background. This is where you curl your legs up underneath you and nestle your back into the soft cushions of an oversized couch. The armrests are slightly worn from other visitors, but for these minutes, or even hours—this spot is yours.

Of course, we don't need a specific destination to be present for life; we only need alert attention. We need to be the watchful presence that witnesses our lives as they unfold one moment after another, and thereby agree to purposefully inhabit our own beings. Unfortunately, days, weeks, and months pass by in a blur as so many people submit to the illusion that going far in life is more essential than going *deep*. Wisdom, meaning, and serenity give way as those with eyes half-closed refuse to live consciously.

As technology speeds us forward, as the workplace winds us up, and as family togetherness moves from the kitchen table to a Happy Meal at a soccer game, some places stand as ensigns to remind us that life is to be relished one delicious swallow at a time.

Even if you don't go for the coffee, try the caramel apple cider on a cold winter day, but don't forget your notebook. Oh, and be sure to curl up on the couch.

4

Higher Consciousness

Confusion

UPON CAREFUL EXAMINATION, WE COME
to the realization that most of our internal bondage originates from a very deep source—the mind. The mind is a
miraculous entity, and though it has the capacity to create
joy and freedom for us, it can just as easily create pain and
bondage.

The mind is the control center for our lives. It
is where we take in information, process it, and devise a
response, thus causing us to participate as co-creators in
the world around us. Life is never happening to us. We
help to create each of our experiences, our relationships,

and the situations we encounter. Every choice we make is inseparably connected to our perception.

Unfortunately, the matchless power of the mind goes unclaimed by us most of the time. We may wonder why our lives are not as we desire, but we rarely take the time to examine the point of origin from which our life extends. Just as we would observe the workings of a watch to ensure it was telling the correct time, we must also scrutinize the workings of our own mind to ensure that it is pointing us to actual reality. However, many of us do not do this. We exist in a state of "wakeful unconsciousness," in that we are physically awake but mentally asleep. We remain unaware that we are victimized by long-established paradigms and destructive thought patterns that imprison us in dysfunction and turmoil.

These thought patterns rule the *thinking mind*. The thinking mind produces a constant recirculation of thoughts. Most of these thoughts have been programmed by the past, which results in destructive mental patterns flowing on an automatic track through our heads. These thought patterns yield insecurity, fear, turmoil, anxiety, negativity, judgment, and confusion—just to name a few.

The thinking mind is easily conditioned to patterns of dysfunction. When snow melts from the top of a mountain, gravity pulls the water down well-worn pathways of ease to the bottom. Our thinking mind operates much the same way. When we encounter a new situation, our thoughts are pulled along prior conditioned pathways that have become imbedded into our thought patterns. Lazily, the mind returns to familiar habits, even ones that we established in the primary years of our existence.

When we begin to pay attention to the workings of our minds, we notice how often they run automatically. We recognize how one thought enters the stage of the mind and then drags us along on a train of thoughts that goes on and on with no determined direction. It is similar to a merry-go-round that runs constantly in circles, forcing us to rethink the same thoughts over and over. The thinking mind often runs on its automatic track when we perform mundane tasks such as driving, cleaning, showering, or preparing dinner. It also runs at night as we lie awake, unable to stop the incessant thoughts streaming through our heads.

Unfortunately, the untrained mind quickly turns destructive. It is out of control when we relive past events that cause us to become upset or agitated or when we mentally project ourselves into the future and become anxious, even though a particular event may be days or weeks away. It sabotages us when we encounter serious problems and our thinking becomes irregular, fear-based, and ineffective. The thinking mind and its habits impede our ability to access higher wisdom. Instead of going to God for answers, our attention merely skims the surface of an ill-effective mind.

This perpetuates emotional strife because untrained thoughts create flares of turbulent emotions.

The thoughts and emotions feed on each other, plunging us in a downward spiral of negativity. Thus after an hour, or even a few minutes, of the thinking mind operating by itself, we are now more worried, more fearful, or more anxious than we were in the beginning, and we are not any closer to a peaceful or a freedom-based solution. Our own minds have just sabotaged us.

These stealthy but powerful thought patterns may go unrecognized by us for years, possibly our whole lives. Over time, they produce a blueprint of mental captivity that is deeply ingrained within us. Even when we encounter brand new situations or relationships, they are all pulled into the mind's old prisons, and we unknowingly create a new version of the same old results. Unconsciously, we blame circumstances, other people, or even life in general for the fact that we are stressed out, in pain, disappointed, or failing again.

In *As A Man Thinketh*, James Allen states that "a particular train of thought, be it good or bad, cannot fail to produce its results on the character and circumstances. A man cannot directly choose his circumstances, but he can choose his thoughts, and so indirectly, yet surely, shape his circumstances."[6]

At first, harmful thought patterns may be difficult to identify, yet the emotions they produce are easier to recognize. Because emotions are closer to the surface of our awareness, we can detect the pain, fear, resentment, or other uncomfortable feelings with greater ease.

These painful emotions serve as signals to us that say, "Go deeper and find the source." The source is often the habitual, destructive patterns of the thinking mind.

Fortunately for us, the thinking mind does not represent the actual power of our minds at all. Deeper than the thinking mind resides our *consciousness*. Consciousness is the connection of intelligence that we share with God, and it is our deepest source of wisdom. When our consciousness takes possession of our thought patterns, we become masterful stewards over our lives. Our choices become purposeful, and we are no longer reactive to situations or to people, and ultimately it leads us to solutions that will free us from suffering.

The relationship between the thinking mind and consciousness is similar to a tablecloth and a table. The thinking mind is like a tablecloth that changes for different seasons. On festive occasions, it is bright and colorful; at dismal times, it is dark and muted. Like the tablecloth, our internal thoughts are reactive to the external circumstances in which we find ourselves. In optimal circumstances, our thoughts are positive and peaceful. In difficult circumstances, they may turn negative and self-sabotaging.

While the thinking mind is like a tablecloth, consciousness is like a table. Just as the table is the solid structure underneath an ever-changing cloth, consciousness is the solid presence underneath the thinking mind. Again, consciousness is the intelligence that we share with God, our mental link to Him. Flowing beneath the thinking mind, it is the ever-present stream of wisdom that will reveal the core truth about ourselves, our relationships, and the situations we encounter.

Like most things of value, consciousness takes effort to access. Unlike the thinking mind, it does not operate without our effort and awareness. It is more like a vehicle waiting patiently to be driven. When consciousness is in the driver's seat, we direct our thought patterns— and thus our lives—as we choose. A deeper dimension, it is only available to us through our concerted focus.

Most people seem to successfully transcend their thinking minds when there are no outside sounds and visual distractions. Here is an example from a friend of mine:

> I had been stressed over finances for months. I was mentally burdened by worry and anxiety and constantly trying to "figure out" what to do. One evening, I was about to turn on the television like I usually do to relax myself, and I decided to sit quietly on the couch instead. I closed my eyes and began to intently focus on my situation. After a few minutes, a sentence emerged in my mind. *You are creating your burden.* Upon inspection, I realized that I was trying to prove my worth by my possessions. Because I needed them to feel good about myself, I was desperately attached to material things. Even after I would get something new, I'd immediately begin looking forward to the next purchase. I was in bondage, because

I had to have things that I didn't actually have money for.

I knew that if I would downgrade my lifestyle I would increase my own freedom, and for the first time, I wasn't afraid of doing so. I felt that even as my possessions shifted, an inner sense of self worth and peace would remain with me. I was in awe at how I had been creating this burden for most of my life but had not been fully aware of it. Yet I was the most influenced by the deep sense of peace and wholeness that I began to feel. —Name Withheld Upon Request

Like the tablecloth blocks the view of the actual table, the thinking mind blocks our ability to access consciousness, our highest level of thinking. When a person is unaware of the solid structure underneath the cloth, the fabric becomes their only reality. Similarly, thoughts produce a pretend reality, a drama, which plays so frequently that we rarely get a true glimpse into the vast dimension of our divine consciousness.

The thought-produced drama in our minds is like a fictional movie. When we watch a movie in a theatre, we sit directly in front of an enormous screen that flashes colorful and alluring images. The sound effects are loud; the music is captivating. We become engaged in the story, and it is almost as though we *are* the story. We are excited, saddened, frustrated, or scared by it. For a brief time, it becomes reality, and we forget that our lives and the drama are actually separate entities.

What we don't realize is that this happens in our minds every day. The thinking mind mentally projects us into the future, or it causes us to relive the past. The past and the future are nothing but fictitious versions of drama, because neither of them actually exist. They are thought forms that parade about as reality. These thought forms pretend to be more important than they actually are, and they drag our attention, or our half- attention, along with the façade. Of course, the only reality is the present time, but when our minds are absorbed by illusion, we are ineffective and ill at ease in the present moment. Until we observe the workings of the thinking mind and bring our attention back to the present time, we rarely become rooted in wise action.

As we step away from this mental conditioning, we begin to recognize that we are not our problems, our fears, or the drama in our heads. The thoughts are the drama, and we—spiritual and conscious beings—merely witness them unfold. We also come to the realization that because we are spirit beings born of God, we have access to a dimension of intelligence that is deeper than this mortal body or its ill-effective mind patterns and problems.

Our first exposure to this concept may be diffi-cult to fully grasp. It is contrary to what we have assumed to be true for most of our lives. It is like someone telling us that a tablecloth isn't really a solid structure when we have never actually seen a table. The surprise we would feel in taking off the cloth for the first time and seeing it as separate from the table is similar to the astonishment we feel when we discover the difference between our consciousness and our thinking minds.

Because some thought patterns are so deeply entrenched within us, we have come to believe that our thoughts and feelings are accurate representations of who we really are. Mistakenly, we conclude:

"I am insecure."

"I am stressed."

"I am negative."

"I am frustrated."

Though we could change the last word of every one of the above sentences or add a million others, "I am" is the only invariable. If the negativity comes and goes, then it isn't us. If fear comes and goes, then it cannot be us. Because we are *eternal* beings, nothing that is temporary can represent who we really are.

On the contrary, the only constant of the thinking mind is that it *always* changes. Fear, negativity, and insecurity come and go as mental thought patterns disguised as reality. However, this is the actual truth:

I am not the insecurity. "I am" is the wholeness that lies beneath my insecurity.

I am not the stress. "I am" is a calm, solid presence underneath the stress.

I am not the negativity. "I am" is watching a habitually negative thought pattern.

I am not the frustration. "I am" is behind the frustration.

Once we fully understand that our identity does not come from our life situation in the physical realm, we free ourselves from the damaging illusion that what we think, feel, and experience represents who we really are. As we step fully into our eternal identity or our own individual "I am," we are not as easily pulled into our temporary problems or our problematic ways of thinking and feeling. From this elevated perspective, we can maneuver ourselves through them more quickly and with greater wisdom.

Higher consciousness is achieved when we merge our intelligence with God's world, not our world. As we awaken, we grow out of our unconscious mind patterns and its subsequent pain and problems. Just as a child grows out of juvenile behaviors, we eventually expand beyond our self-created prisons and enter a new existence that is abundant in truth, freedom, and peace.

5

At the Edge of Infinity

Pain

THE OAK TREE SHED ITS LEAVES CARELESSLY onto the sidewalk of my grandmother's house. As my brother pulled his car under its cascading branches, I looked through the windshield and saw my father. He was on the porch of the same alcoholic home he'd left in a hurry thirty years ago. He wasn't inside, but he couldn't remove himself from the property; his life echoed a similar story.

After thirteen years of abstinence, my father had recently regressed to life as an active alcoholic. However, this time, he had the added vice of prescription drugs. This warm day in August, my brother and I had come to give him a ride from our grandmother's house to his own house, which was thirty minutes away.

My brother got out of the car and motioned him toward us. I stayed seated. I felt the sickness again. It was a giant, formidable ball of some dense substance that took residence in my throat and seeped into my chest every time I had seen or spoken to him in the last three years. I tried to ignore it, but it seized me in his presence every time.

As he approached us, I finally climbed out of the car and stood in front of him. He appeared to be a shell of the father that I had once known. Previously full of life, his eyes now drooped low, the lids partially closed. His black hair, badly in need of a cut, had grown over his ears and brushed his eyebrows. His facial creases were deeper than I remembered, and the thick, dark stubble on his chin bore witness of neglect. His voice was deep and raspy, his speech erratic. As I reached up to hug him, I was torn between hesitation and desperate longing in one sweeping embrace.

He had come back to his childhood town, thirty minutes away from his actual residence, to obtain drugs from a new physician. He had burned through his welcome with his old doctor, who had just given him an entire month's prescription seven days ago. It was already gone, and he needed another source. The new doctor penned him a prescription for twelve more pills, though he didn't have a dime with which to buy them. As we drove home, he asked my brother and me for money, but we both declined to give him any. Neither ten nor ten thousand dollars was what he truly needed. I felt helpless, but in my mind, I believed I had only one thing to give that might make a difference.

It was the truth. Yet this was a completely new venture for me. Despite our recent estrangement, we had always claimed a special affinity for one another. Actually, we hardly knew each other at all. I longed for his affection, so for years I played the part of an adoring daughter, but I could only do this with my eyes closed against a harsh reality. I now feared that if I continued to follow the script blindly, our little play would end at his grave. On this warm afternoon, I felt older than I ever had in front of him, and with the grace of God, I amassed enough courage to speak the truth I had agreed for so long never to say.

As my brother sped the car along the highway, I turned to face him in the backseat. I explained that I knew of his addictions and did not believe he would overcome them on his own. I addressed several lies he had recently told me and insisted he stop manipulating me through deceit. I explained that I loved him dearly, but his behavior was withering our relationship, which had only a handful of life left. My words cut through a lifetime of deception, and my palms shook as the sounds tumbled forth from my mouth. A gushing river of truth flowed through a newly opened gate of permission, surging forward before my carefully trained mind could command it to stop. At the end of my eruption, I told him I'd try to find a treatment center if he would agree to go.

As I spoke, he reclined his whole body across the back seat and lay there silently looking at the ceiling. When I finished, his response was that he had a plan to overcome his problems, and he didn't need help to do it. There was no part of me that could believe him.

When we arrived at the house where he was staying, he stepped out of the car and rambled up the sidewalk. As we drove away, there were pieces of my heart scattered all over the ground like pebbles.

Fortunately, that night he suffered from intense drug withdrawals and called me asking for help the next morning. I spent much of that day researching prospective treatment centers and contacting the doctors' offices he had circulated. When I explained how much medication he had taken, one of the nurses informed me that he was in a life-threatening stage of detoxification and advised me to take him to the emergency room immediately.

I called my father. I explained her recommendations and to my surprise, he agreed to go. However, when I asked for instructions to his house, he didn't know them. He knew that he lived near an alley close to a church downtown, but he didn't know the name of the street. As I drove to pick him up, I tried to follow his approximate directions while remembering the route we had taken the night before, but still I wandered aimlessly. I meandered through alleyways close to the main roads I remembered, fearing for his life all the while. The inexplicable but tangible sickness had seized my insides once again. I was certain I had aged several years in a matter of days.

After driving for some time, a voice in my head told me to leave the street I was on and turn the opposite direction. Just then, I saw him crossing the road fifty yards ahead of me. When I reached him, I rolled down my window and asked him to get in. He looked at me with surprise and asked, "Are we going somewhere?"

I reminded him that we were going to the emergency room, and he willingly climbed in the car. We drove around for awhile, looking for the house he was renting. When we finally arrived, he invited me in, but I declined. I met one of his roommates the day before, and I was uncomfortable just being in the driveway. I sat in the car with the radio off and waited with the doors locked. I thought I might cry, but my eyes were as dense as the concrete lodged in my chest. I drew in breaths slowly, deliberately, while I stared at the front door of his house.

Ten minutes later he emerged with a cardboard box full of the few items he still possessed from multiple moves in a few months time. He told me it was all that he owned.

On the way to the hospital, he used familiar, well-played tactics to win my affection. He spoke of how he needed me and trusted me, but his words had lost their meaning. It was like watching an old movie when you've memorized every line. Hearing them again increased my agony. I loved him deeply, almost desperately, and I knew that he really did love me. I had the distant memory of many good qualities that had once existed in the withered form of a man who now sat beside me. Yet I couldn't bring them into view. Feelings of nausea oozed through my stomach and tightness gripped my chest. I remained mostly silent as I drove, gaping open and bleeding on the inside.

When we arrived, I clambered out of the car and stood in front of the hospital with the man that fathered me and fumbled at raising me. I stared at the clouds and the sky began to spin. Something inexplicable was happening in my mind. The heavy, solid block lodged in my core was unwinding—first inches at a time and seconds later, by miles. Twenty-five years of denial was uncoiling faster and faster as two and a half decades began to whirl before my vision . . . the façade of our relationship . . . the claim of loving me . . . the years of estrangement . . . the pretense of parenting . . . the gripping nausea . . . the pain I couldn't face . . . the repetitious words . . . the belonging I ached for. It was all unraveling. I closed my eyes and lowered my head to ground myself. The spinning slowed, and the earth stood still just long enough for me to understand what all of the universe had just agreed to release to me.

He sacrificed me.

It was a reality I had suspected, but simply refused to accept before that day. He traded a real relationship with me for other things—alcohol, work, friends, marriages, hobbies, drugs, even sports. There it was. The secret was out. I inhaled my first deep breath in two days.

For me the ultimate prize of belonging had always been from him, but I could never win it for long. Though there were some good times in our relationship, they were overshadowed by cavernous gaps of estrangement. As a child, I tried so hard to win his attention, but I never could secure more than weekend pats on the head. I felt he didn't really want me. Why? What had I done? Though other people in my life loved me, somehow their love could not erase this handicap of rejection I carried. It lived furtively under my skin and spread through my body like a secret, silent tumor.

We walked slowly toward the hospital, and though the loyalist in me wanted to go in, the rest of me could not consent. I was still such a child when it came to him—still wounded by his rejection and immature in my capacity. I could not take on a fully adult role of trying to save him anymore today.

Dichotomy tore through me. I loved him, and I loathed him in the same instant. I desperately needed him, yet I couldn't stand to be with him. The pain in the afternoon wind whipped through me, caved my chest, and made it hard to breathe. Fortunately, my husband

and children needed me home and gave me a legitimate cover for the real reason I could not stay. So I left.

I left the parking lot and released him to the hands of God, the only hands that could truly save him now. I wondered if I would ever see him alive again, and I offered a feeble prayer that I exhaled to Heaven for both of us. Though I was unsure of his fate, I believed that the prayer for me would come to pass in some distant day. I asked that we would both be healed from our pain and finally come to wholeness, freedom, and peace.

Until this time, I was so afraid of pain that I did anything to avoid feeling it. I blocked it out of my mind or distracted myself with accomplishment—if I could just *do* enough good things, then maybe I wouldn't *feel* so badly. I used work, achievements, and other people like drugs to numb the pain I couldn't face. When all of my efforts turned up empty, I would beg God to ease my unhappiness.

I had given a gold-medal attempt at avoiding pain. Yet just after this visit home, a lifetime of repressed feelings rose from the other side of eternity and begged for reconciliation. Fortunately by now, I knew running offered no solace. It is impossible to run away from yourself, because you eventually show up wherever you go. The past pain we carry in our inner crevices will surge through to our present relationships. We can't help but bring it with us. It lies dormant in our mental framework and our emotional memories waiting to be awakened to life when touched by any new stimulus. Unless we face our pain and follow the full path of healing, we will always live under the shadow of its dark ceilings.

Now that I was finally ready to begin the journey, I began to write authentically about my thoughts and feelings. One line at a time, I tried to persuade out of exile what I had repressed for so many years by building a relationship to the pain. Of this necessity, in *The Power of Focusing*, Ann Weiser Cornell states:

> Being in a relationship with your inner experience allows you to be **with** your feelings, not **in** them. Many people think that the only way to change strong emotions is to jump right into the middle of them, feel them intensely, and get **through** them . . . When you have a relationship with what's there, you are able to be its listener. It is able to tell you its story. If you **are** it, then there is no one else to hear the story. This inner relationship is how you give yourself the healing presence that is so powerful and helpful. If you find yourself saying, "I am sad," try changing that to . . . **"I'm aware of something that feels sad."** Now the sad feeling becomes something you can **be with** instead of feeling all over because it's part of you, not all of you.[7]

As I became aware of painful feelings, they usually carried some type of physical sensation, and I learned to center my attention completely on what I felt. Much of the time, I only had to become inwardly still, focus intently, and eventually a message would be revealed to me. It seemed as though the child that I used to be only needed the adult woman to understand a certain message, and once I did, the pain would depart.

On a few occasions, I felt that addressing certain people openly about the past helped me to heal particular grievances. Then there were other times that I could not mend my own wounds, and I had to lay them at the feet of Deity and request to be healed. Our deepest place of wisdom can direct us to the most effective path of healing for us in each circumstance.

Unfortunately, in the face of painful emotion, most people choose one of two ineffective courses. Some insert themselves completely into what they feel, and in a sense, they wear the emotion around, though really it is wearing *them* around. The emotion takes on a life of its own and the person becomes irrational, often acting out whatever they feel. As they become reactive to their feelings, logic subsides and they can easily get beyond the reach of reason. Instead of healing their emotions, they are detoured by them.

On the opposite side of the spectrum, others will place an inner wall of resistance between themselves and their pain, believing this will protect them from discomfort. In an effort to be strong, they become emotionally hardened, and at times disconnected from themselves and others. Yet the pain they fear, and therefore resist, still exists behind the walls they've constructed. Despite their protective measures, they suffer anyway as they become inadvertently controlled by what they refuse to address.

Conscious awareness of our emotions is the most effective means of coping with pain. It is when we address our feelings, rather than resist them. It is when we become aware of them, but not immersed in them. We listen to their messages in order to extract wisdom, but we remain focused on freedom and healing. Daniel Goleman teaches:

> Self awareness is not an attention that gets carried away by emotions, overreacting and amplifying what is perceived. Rather, it is a neutral mode that maintains self-reflectiveness even amidst turbulent emotions . . . At a minimum, it manifests itself simply as a slight stepping-back from experience, a parallel stream of consciousness that is . . . hovering above or beside the main flow, aware of what is happening rather than being immersed and lost in it.[8]

This self-awareness that he speaks of allows us to significantly raise our consciousness of our inner emotional states and know how to deal with them effectively rather than destructively. It also helps us avoid the temptation to become stuck in the story of our past or to create a victim identity out of our pain. Victims build their own prisons, and they mistakenly believe they can't be released until other people set them free. Conscious awareness of emotion dictates that we do not address past pain to hide in it—only to heal it.

We must be willing not only to begin this process,

but see it through to its conclusion. During my path of healing, I learned to accept each stage of the process. In the beginning, there were times I wondered if I'd drown in the contents of a well of anger and sorrow that seemed to have no end. After that initial period of cleansing passed, I spent many hours in stillness and reflection where I learned volumes about my inner workings. Of course, the most important stage of the process was the final one, when I came to Jesus Christ and asked to be healed. If my Eternal Father possessed infinite wisdom and perfect power, why should I agree to remain broken because of other human beings? As His eternal child, I was not damaged goods as I once suspected. I was just in the middle of a process and we—my God and myself—weren't finished yet.

As I learned to access infinite power through prayer and faith in Jesus Christ, He slowly began to re-create me. One ounce at a time, He exchanged the anguish I carried for tranquility. He replaced my pain with understanding. He showed me that the love and belonging that I sought from others, I already had with Him. In time, peace began to ebb gently through my old crevices as forgiveness washed them clean and closed my gaps.

The unexpected result was that I began to take residence in my own being. Because I no longer repressed and denied whole sections of my life, I narrowed the space between who I was and who I really wanted to be. I was no longer operating from pain or fear; I was just operating. I was open to the truth of myself and my life in the splendor of its full authenticity. I felt I had traveled to the outer edge of infinity, and when I came back, all of me was home.

As human beings, we are meant to be whole, although it is hard to remember that when giant pieces of our lives crumble apart and crash to the ground. In our human existence, we will each have experiences that crush us and cause us excruciating pain. We are not meant to run away or bury our feelings in deep, inner holes, forcing us to carry emotional aches forever. We are meant to address the pain and in doing so, be transformed by it. In the pursuit of health and well-being, it is our responsibility to heal the past and then release it.

We each have an ideal life formula to create the best version of ourselves, and healing our pain is a vital step that can catapult us to our highest realm. If we don't process it, we remain torn, injured, and separated from our wholeness. Only partially complete, we are trapped in transition, unable to capture the perfection of the finished product.

The Great Creator fully understands how to obtain perfect end results with His creations, yet we do not. We shouldn't say, "Why me?" but rather, "Teach me." We must trust that if we begin the process and pursue it to completion, we will eventually step beyond the seemingly impenetrable ceilings of struggle that prevent our growth and enter a state of wholeness.

Eighteen months after our encounter at the hospital, my father died of a prescription drug overdose. I have reflected on that specific prayer that I released to God that afternoon, and in our unique way, I know my request has been granted for both of us. We have both been "healed from our pain, and come to a place of wholeness, compassion, and peace." His came by returning home; mine came by healing.

When we sorted through my father's belongings, they fit into that same cardboard box he carried with him on that warm summer day to the hospital. Of his possessions, I received a half-empty bottle of olive oil, a Bible with some pages ripped from its binding, and two paisley printed ties. Pain, though unintentional, was one of his more important offerings to me.

I am uncommonly blessed to receive the gifts that came from its unsteady hands. I faced uncertainty, but created stability. I knew anger, but experienced forgiveness. I waded through pain, but understood peace. I was injured, but I learned wholeness. I lost my earthly father, but through it, I found my Eternal One.

All fathers leave something to their children, and my father left me a path on which I could create more of myself.

I will always bless his name because of it.

6

Opening to Life
Control

THE DESERT SUN BEAT DOWN ON US WITH an unusual blare for eight o'clock in the morning. Besides myself, there was just one other family at the pool enjoying the calm water before a crowd of people armed with alligator-shaped flotation devices, ice coolers, and vibrant colored beach towels flooded through the gates and sprawled onto the cement deck to sizzle like eggs in the sun.

At that moment, my husband, David, was home flipping pancakes, cleaning spilled orange juice, and calming young cries. I sat with a book in my hands in front of the clear blue water, graciously lapping up his gift of solitude for one precious hour on a Saturday morning. My reading, however, was soon interrupted as the angry voice of a man in the pool invaded my ears. I looked up and noticed that he was teaching his young daughter, about eight years old, to swim.

I watched them for a moment and immediately recognized his vital error as an instructor. It's against the law of gravity to swim a front crawl with your head and shoulders out of the water. With an elevated torso, your legs fall naturally to the ground below you. His misguided attempt was an adaptation to her fear, or terror rather, of burying her face into the water, which is the easiest way to render your body horizontal.

He commanded her to swim to the wall. She tried, but couldn't. His voice rose in chastisement, casting a blanket of tension upon us. She tried again, but once more, she failed.

He then carried her from the wall into the middle of the pool and backed away from her, leaving her alone in the water, extremely heightening her panic. Like a cat being thrown into a lake, stiff and horrified, she tried to swim another time. I watched intently. Even the groundskeeper seemed to be cheering her on, but she failed again—and every time after that.

In arms three times the size of her own, he picked her up and threw her around in the water. He was tense and angry, but trying to cover it through the pretense of play. He was a poor actor. Even I could feel his disdain.

Finally, she began to cry, her small body's only defense against his well-intentioned tyranny. She walked away from him toward her mother who sat on the steps of the pool. He stood alone, hip deep in water, inhaling great breaths with a tightened jaw. As her mother wrapped her arm around the girl's shoulder, his voice bellowed towards them and he questioned tensely, "Sierra, *what's wrong?*"

"What *is* wrong?" Peace begs for an answer to that question as tension has now escalated into a cultural epidemic. We constantly find ourselves immersed in its clutches—at work, in our relationships, or even with complete strangers. For many, tension has become a steady state of being, and only on occasion do we enjoy brief interludes of tranquility that break the constant flow of stress that we encounter. As spiritual seekers, we must wonder if this is truly the way that we were meant to live. Surely, we know that it isn't. Nevertheless, stress and tension are such common parts of life that we fail to question the madness that constantly surrounds us.

A main catalyst for the tension we feel within us is our resistance to what is undesirable in our lives. We naturally want to resist or deny what we don't like, because a part of us believes if we refuse to accept that thing, it might change. However, we cannot change what actually *is* in the very moment it occurs. We can resist the cashier who is slow, but he will still work as he chooses. We can resist the disease, but we still have it. We can resist the fact that we're behind schedule, but we still show up late. Most of the time, it is our resistance to reality, not reality itself that creates the tension that we feel.

Rather than seeking to control life, it is better to let life live through us. This is allowing ourselves to completely accept the things we are unable to change so we do not cultivate tension as we experience them. Opening is for the daughter who is afraid to swim, the person driving 25 mph in a 45 mph zone, or the one we love who betrays us. Simply speaking, opening to life is offering no emotional or mental resistance to what we cannot control in our lives. It does not mean that we condone that particular thing, nor does it mean that we will not take action to change what *is* within our power. It is to inwardly yield to the unchangeable reality—that it exists.

In *The Power of Now*, Tolle teaches that we should

> . . . accept (the) here and now totally by dropping all inner resistance. The false, unhappy self that loves feeling miserable, resentful, or sorry for itself can then no longer survive. This is called surrender. Surrender is not weakness. There is great strength in it . . . Through surrender, you will be free internally of the situation.[9]

When our family moved to the East Coast, I quickly learned the wisdom of surrendering. Having relocated from a small city in Idaho to Pittsburgh,

Pennsylvania—a place full of tunnels, bridges, and poorly planned highways—I soon gained a new understanding of the phrase "traffic jam." In Idaho, ten cars backed up behind a snow plow is not an authentic traffic problem (though one might wonder while watching the reaction of some of the drivers). A real traffic jam is when cars are backed up from downtown to the suburbs with drivers sunbathing on their roofs and passing bags of Doritos across the highway.

Having sat in more highway stops than should be legal, I learned how sensible opening to life really is. Though a roomful of people may be waiting for me, their teacher, to show up, I must accept the fact that my lane of traffic will not move forward, even if I were to exert all of my will to demand it. The driver next to me may honk, curse, or pull his hair with frustration, but we both remain exactly where we are.

Tara Bennet-Goleman teaches,

> This quality of being attuned to and surrendering to the mood of the present is invaluable in dealing with emotions. Some things in life can't be changed, but we can change our inner relationship to them. Accepting their presence mindfully helps us hold even roiling emotions with a depth of spirit, a soulful wisdom.[10]

Surrendering to what we cannot change aids in the process of opening to life. To live in a state of equanimity in the midst of difficult situations, the practice of opening must occur in both the mind and the body. We open our minds because this is where we perceive a situation and choose how to deal with it. We open our bodies because that is where tension takes residence within us and where we continue to carry it. Through concentration and deep breathing, we can bring the body and the mind again to a peaceful state. Our problem may still exist, but instead of acting out the stress, we can wisely step back and know how to address it.

If we openly accept life, we may wonder if we'll become spineless, ineffective, or perhaps lose control of our lives. Yet if we look carefully, we see that the opposite is true. When we accept what we can't change, we are free to focus all of our mental power on what we *can* change. (How does resisting a traffic jam make us more effective anyway?) When we can do something about a situation, all of our efforts become streamlined into wise action that stems from a state of equanimity. When we cannot do anything, we accept what we cannot change. Instead of creating unnecessary stress and tension, we maintain a clear mind and a peaceful soul, watching carefully for the choices that we can take hold of to create our lives as we desire them to be.

Life is very much like a river that rushes downstream. It is peaceful to watch the natural flow of the water. This is exactly what the river was meant to do. Imagine that a person wants to change its direction, so he carries an armful of bricks into the middle of the riverbed and tries to stack them up. However, each time a brick is inserted into the water, it yields to the flow of the current and tumbles away.

In frustration, the man tries again and again to make a wall, but his menial efforts never change the direction of the water. After each attempt, he would only become increasingly tense and aggravated. Only a fool would continue this process, because in the laws of nature, a river flows freely in its intended course.

In the laws of nature, *life* also flows freely. Life will continue to flow with or without our consent. If we put up an inner wall of resistance to the things we cannot control, they still knock us over and make us angry as we tumble. However, when we accept them, we create a peaceful and wise space for them to pass through. Again, it is our resistance to the problem, not the problem itself that generates tension. Acceptance of what we can't change means that we agree to meet life where it actually is, not where a mentally constructed paradigm thinks it ought to be. This heals us from the anxiety we feel in the space between what we want to happen and what actually is happening. When we close that space, the tension dissipates.

Just after my husband and I had children, I soon recognized that I would exert strong, internal resistance toward certain situations that I was unable to control. If one of our children would cry in a store for something he couldn't have, resistance measures would activate within my body. My jaw would become tense, my chest would tighten, and it even seemed that my vision would narrow. Tension is uncomfortable, even painful to feel. It speaks loudly and irrationally and urges us to respond instantaneously. When we're under its influence, we'd do anything to get the stimulus to bend to our will, which usually results in some form of mistreatment of the person we happen to be resisting.

Over time, I learned that if I first inwardly acknowledged what the child was doing the very moment they were doing it, I could create enough space to respond wisely. *Then* I would act. Often, I still chose to discipline—at times firmly—but my behavior was not an immediate emotional reaction to the tension I felt. Instead, acceptance opened a space that allowed me to act in the wisest manner.

Child rearing has become a constant place for me to practice opening to life. One afternoon my two oldest boys and I were baking together when one of them mistakenly dumped half of a chocolate cake mix onto the floor. I paused to look at the mess. It was already there, and we were well beyond altering that reality. (It's madness to live in resistance to accidents.) I calmly instructed him how to properly hold the bag next time to avoid a reoccurrence, and I asked him to get the broom and clean the floor. As he was sweeping up the mess, my other son questioned me, "Aren't you going to yell?"

The guilty party holding the dustpan answered, "You know, she really doesn't yell that much anymore."

Apparently, miracles still happen. Even though I have many miles to go, acceptance of what *is* has allowed me to tread a few feet on the path of peace.

After we let go of our desire to control the outside world, we can fully return to the inner world that demands our attention. This is the only part of the universe where we need to maintain power. Here, we constantly choose to be captain of our internal environment or captive to our external one.

When we open ourselves and accept the rushing waters of life, we can be assured that we will still be standing triumphantly as they pass through. When we close the doors, struggling to maintain illusory control, our opposition ensures that life will beat upon us wildly.

We do not need to control all the elements around us to yield a beautiful, sunny day. The sky doesn't have to be clear for us to feel tranquil. Underneath ballooning clouds of rain or in the middle of driving snow, we are free when we realize that peace is not a place we have to locate, but simply a choice that we have to make.

From my lounge chair, I watched Sierra as she sat on the steps, crying uncontrollably. Tears brimmed on the edge of my own eyelids for her unnecessary pain. She could not do what her father demanded, and he met her tender fears with tension and control. It defeated her and she gave up altogether.

After several minutes, his anger finally subdued and a look of bewilderment spread across his face. Slowly he walked through the water and stood beside his daughter. He turned to her mother and said, "What should I do?"

I answered his question quietly. *Do not seek to control her. Insert yourself into the flow of who she is and not who you demand her to be. Then you will live in peace with your child and know best how to guide her.*

7

Right Where You're Standing

Denial

I WAS BORN SELFISH. PERHAPS IT CAME WITH my human packaging, just like my hazel eyes and brown hair. It may once have been dismissed as the ordinary nature of a young child, but a twenty-three-year-old woman demanding her way is more alarming than a toddler throwing a fit over a toy.

In a culture that frowns upon selfishness, I tried to hide it as I would dirty clothes under my bed during room inspection. Nevertheless "out of sight, out of mind" doesn't take anything out of existence. Filthy socks and selfish deeds pushed into the shadows just multiply in the darkness and eventually resurface, reeking for reconciliation. Denying my selfishness did not make it disappear. Defending my behavior in front of others didn't prevent them from seeing it, and shaming myself couldn't make me stop doing it.

After I had exhausted all my options, I finally took a deep breath of character, bent down very low, and peered under the mattress to see what I had pushed into the darkness. I was alarmed to realize just how much old laundry needed to be addressed.

In a moment of grace, I chose ownership over denial, and I embraced the truth of what actually *was*. Ownership turned the lights on, and I was finally able to perceive myself with clarity. Over time, I learned to recognize selfishness as it rose up inside of me, and I recalled its familiar voice, as well as its consequences. Eventually, I even became amused by its continual beckoning, but again and again, I simply chose not to follow its call. When I slipped, ownership placed me again in the commanding seat of my own choices.

Debbie Ford teaches that ownership is when we "acknowledge that a quality belongs to (us). Now we can begin to take responsibility for all of who we are, the parts we like and the parts we dislike."[11]

She continues,

> *Taking responsibility is a huge task. Most of us are willing to take responsibility for the good we create in our lives, but we often resist taking responsibility for the bad. When we take responsibility, we can be*

*empowered by everything . . . This is the place of power
from which you can alter your life.*[12]

Somewhere in my development, I adopted the practice of loathing myself for what was undesirable in my character. It was as though one part of me had declared war on another and tried to force it into submission through abhorrence and shame, causing me to live as one house divided.

The truth can be a difficult thing to embrace, especially when it doesn't make us look as fabulous as we feel we ought to appear. When we want the formal living spaces of our lives to be clean and free of unwanted character clutter, we take our personal junk and throw it into dark, deep closets for hiding. Sometimes, even *we* don't realize what we've shoved behind the door. However, our commitment to wholeness brings with it a responsibility to tell the truth. We must turn the handle of every basement door, dig through the attic, look under the beds, and claim, "All of this junk is mine."

In order to become whole, we have to take full possession of the human structure that is our own. We must tell the whole truth and nothing but the truth.

"I am selfish."

"I am jealous."

"I am unforgiving."

"I am insecure."

"I am addicted."

Dysfunction operates freely under the blanket of denial, but ownership helps us see things as they really are. Not until we acknowledge what is, can we change it.

It is impossible to overcome our ceilings until we own their existence. As a directionally challenged traveler, I've learned that besides knowing your final destination, you first must know your starting point. As travelers in humanity, we have to stare hard at the ground resting below our feet and mark it like the big red circle on a map with an X in the middle that says "I am *here*."

A friend of mine once wrote "I have a fear of conflict and a fear of rejection and this leads to problems in my relationships." Her authenticity is her greatest asset. The fact that she knows exactly where she stands is precisely the reason she won't be there long.

Often, we resist the truth about ourselves to avoid the painful feelings that result upon acknowledging the facts. However, resistance ultimately creates more pain than does ownership. It's similar to putting our finger on a hot stove and telling all the people around us—including ourselves—that nothing is burning. When we see the problem, we can stop the pain.

However, resisting what is undesirable is deeply embedded into our culture. We resist pain because we want to feel good. We resist exploring family problems because we want to seem close. We resist our strengths because we want to be humble. We resist our weaknesses because we want to be better than that. We resist our insecurities because we want to be confident. We resist our failures because they hurt. We resist our addictions because we can't stop.

Denial comes with its own adhesive. As long as we refuse to own our personal ceilings, they will maintain their bonded hold on us. The purpose of life is transformation. Therefore, we were meant to overcome our boundaries so that we could create the noblest version of ourselves. If we refuse to recognize our ceilings, God will allow them to reappear in front of us until we are worn down, weary, or humble enough to finally open our eyes. If we refuse to travel the course of transformation, Providence will attempt to help us along.

It is critical that we do not tolerate our boundaries and the pain they cause, and adjust our lives around them. A woman I once knew suffered a shoulder injury from a horseback riding accident. She chose not to pursue full medical treatment and instead maladapted her physical activity around the pain. Even many years after the incident, she was still unable to raise her arms above her shoulders. Because she tolerated the injury day after day, it limited her life and constantly caused her pain.

We cannot be free of our pain until we recognize its source and complete the full process of healing. For example, some people do not fully heal from divorce, and they carry residual pain into their next relationship. Others may not fully heal from suffering that they experienced in childhood, and they bring it with them when they become parents.

In order to be whole beings, we must travel full course, which entails going through the less-than-ideal to get to the ideal. We cannot ignore what is ugly and pretend that we see real beauty, just as we cannot ignore deep pain and authentically lay claim on peace. If we want to love, we need to confront the hatred inside of us before we can heal it. If we desire peace, we have to wade through our trauma before we can reach serenity on the other side. If we seek to have a close family, we must acknowledge the distance between its members before we can bridge it.

As we take accountability for our lives, we grasp the handle on the door of liberty. This door is ours and ours alone to open. We may rightfully fix our gaze on an ideal future, but first we need know right where we're standing. The simple but crucial act of ownership will allow us to step from that spot and walk the path that leads beyond it.

8

Dreaming Well

Fear

TODAY MY SEVEN-YEAR-OLD TOSSED A PENNY into a pool of water and wished aloud for a Star Wars land speeder. He didn't mean the toy. I smiled, rumpled his hair, and kissed the top of his head. I remember how as a girl, I dreamt of flying over the cornfields of the Midwest, and when I awoke, I wished for a flowing red cape. I knew if I had enough pennies and enough intent, one would spontaneously emerge just for me. It never did, but the dream of flying never left me.

Since then, I have been a dreamer whether I am awake or not. In junior high, I was a rock star, in high school, a tennis-pro, and in college, I toured through

Europe on a bicycle. During our first few years of marriage, I likened our relationship to a helium balloon. I was the balloon with my head in the clouds, and my husband was the string attaching us to the ground. Unfortunately, spending so much time where oxygen is sparse had melded "flighty" into my character.

At some point after I had children, reality hit me. I turned into the string and spent a few years tied closely to the ground. Nevertheless, after stability had engrained itself into the rubber soles of my Keds, I knew I was meant to view life from higher than dirt level.

Today I still throw mental pennies into bodies of water, but my wishes are slightly different. I'm old enough to stay in reach of gravity, but optimistic enough to view the future in bright, bold colors. I stopped asking for Superwoman's cape and started envisioning a life teaching spiritual truths—a goal that is challenging, but possibly attainable. Just after my wish for peace on earth, getting through the grocery store without my children breaking any glass items would be greatly appreciated.

Fear is the great boundary that stands between where we are and where we want to go. A few weeks ago, I gave a lecture in which I said, "Courage is not the absence of fear; courage is being afraid and doing it anyway." As I spoke, several people nodded their heads in affirmation. (I love it when they do that.) However, just then, I remembered that the manuscript for my book had been sitting on my desk for three months bound behind a steel railing of fear that would not allow me to release it.

Writing down words on a page is one thing, but handing it over to others is simply terrifying. When one of my friends asked for a rough copy, I tried to hand her the pages, but my fingers would not release their grip. We stood there looking at each other, both of us clutching one side. She laughed and said, "Hard to let go, huh?"

Yes. It's like cracking open your sternum and peeling back your rib cage with both hands to expose your innermost parts to anyone who happens to pass by.

When it comes to our dreams, our grasp must loosen, or we'll always be fenced in by fear. Sometimes we have to be willing to reveal ourselves and just hope the world will treat us gently. It may not. No matter, there are only two front seats in our vehicle—one is for us and the other for God. If fear or popular opinion occupies the seat beside us, there is little ability to be steered by the Divine.

I've learned that not all people are friendly to those who have visions, especially if our visions happen to be larger than theirs are. Some people responded to my publishing aspirations with the same forced tone of encouragement that I use when my son tells me he wants to be an astronaut, a dentist, a singer, and a race car driver, all at the same time. I believe he can accomplish what he diligently works for, and I know reality will settle upon him in its own time. So I'm careful not to break open the cocoon dreams of my children, but should life do it for them, I know that butterflies can still emerge. But, if you break open the dreams of adults, dejected insects just might crawl out. The elasticity of our spirits can escape through our pores with age. In the development stage of our fetal dreams, there are times we need to stop publicly sharing them, so we can protect their growth.

Franklin Delano Roosevelt uttered the famous statement "We have nothing to fear, but fear itself." Nevertheless, we allow ourselves to be driven into a corner of submission by countless elements of terror. We fear loss, we fear risk, we fear rejection, and most certainly, we fear failure. These factors of intimidation may never leave us, but eventually, we have to stand up, command them to step aside, and simply move forward. Being a small woman with large dreams does not create the life of greatest ease. Yet despite the regular pangs of fear, there is a rich satisfaction that swells above and beyond whatever discomfort we may endure.

When working toward our dreams, it is critical to assess our motives. Dreams that originate from the ego or the carnal presence often involve proving ourselves to others. Because they operate from scarcity and have a constant need of validation, these motives are strictly fear-based. We're afraid that we're not enough, and so we use our achievements as a venue to prove that we are. Consequently, joy in our work is solely dependent upon "making it." All satisfaction obtained by the carnal presence is painfully short-lived, because it seeks satisfaction from sources that cannot permanently fill it. The only solution is to abandon our ego instead of placate it.

While the carnal presence works for the sake of validation, the spirit works for the sake of the work itself, because it simply wants to create a life that is meaningful and full of purpose. If our dreams and our work arise from the God-like part of who we are, we find fulfillment throughout the process, because we are not merely holding out for a certain end result. Because we feel whole already, our satisfaction is not derived from being better than others. We feel joy in achieving our own unique potential and happy for those who achieve theirs. We use our efforts to bless other people in the world instead of compete with them.

I have endured a battle with my carnal presence for many years. I have turned it over to God countless times. I have dug a deep grave and tried to push it in. I have learned its thought patterns and tried to cut them off. Though it is dormant most of the time, still I can find no permanent absolution.

I am most often free of my carnal presence when my work flows purely through me. Writing and teaching is a power of creation that comes from God, a Source beyond me, and simply uses me as an instrument to string certain words together. Here, I have nothing to fear, nor do I have anything to prove. On these days, in the periphery of my mind, I see the apparition of a woman in a distant place, like a watermark on a sheet of paper. Today I saw her again, and she looked somewhat like me.

She stood on top of a high mountain surrounded by blue sky, and she stared into a spacious canyon. She had climbed to that place, one slow step after another. The air seemed to hold her motionless as she looked forward in the stillness. Light, symbolizing truth, ran through the center of her chest, seeped into her veins, and pulsed at the point of her fingertips. There is nothing man-made around her. Every piece of her backdrop was held in the palm of God as it was created, and thus it remains. No material concern holds her attention.

She has come with a request for God. So many people suffer. She asks if the truth that originates with Him might come through her and into the planet, allowing her to act as an instrument for healing. She seeks not to be one of the "greats"—just one of the players. She stands as a watermark in my mind, an imprint, bringing a vision to me as I work.

Julia Cameron wrote, "The dreams of my heart are the dreams of the universe dreaming through me. I am a gate for God to accomplish great things . . . I am a portal, an entryway for the grace and power of God to show themselves in the world." [13]

I believe when you declare your intentions to the universe, it will adjust its course to fit you in. As my children pitch copper pennies into the water, just next to them, I throw my own silent coins into a vast dreaming well. Occasionally, I toss in a Susan B. Anthony just to make sure. Though my feet are still on the ground, I observe the earth from an aerial view. Looking down, I can see a small space for my visions and me, and I ask life to bend its course slightly to make room for us.

9

Upward Climb

Defeat

I TURNED THE KNOB TO "IGNITE" AND HEARD the familiar clicking sound of the backyard grill, but no flame burst as a result of my efforts. It was five o' clock, and we had planned our family evening around a barbecue and a sunset. No propane—no sunset dinner.

I heaved the barren barrel into the back of our truck, pulled out of the driveway, and followed my husband's directions to the nearest store that sold propane. Our house rested on the outskirts of a booming city, southeast of Phoenix, and my errands always directed me north, headlong into commercialized bustle. These directions, however, pointed me on a course in the opposite direction.

I had mistakenly believed that south of our neighborhood haven lay only miles of farmland and if you drove far enough, the San Tan Mountains. I drove curiously as I passed orange tree orchards, plots of land-sprouting single-wide trailers, some horse ranches, and finally a taco stand.

In close proximity, I spotted a sign that read "Liquor, Propane, Lottery." The liquor and the lottery I had no use for, but their center compatriot held our hopeful dinner in its hands. Slowly, I pulled into a parking lot that was littered with cigarette butts, aluminum cans, and newspapers. I ambled my vehicle in a wave-like motion to avoid the gaping potholes that stood ready to swallow my tires.

Paint from the walls of the convenient store peeled off in long, finger-like strips that bent towards the earth and dangled dejectedly above the concrete. The advertisement signs hung crookedly next to dirt-spackled windowpanes. The smell of cigarette smoke and chili peppers filled my nostrils. Two other trucks were in line for propane, and both male occupants seemed to have appreciated *all* the services this little store offered. I waited, feeling strangely out of place only ten minutes from my home.

Finally, a large man with bronzed skin and a long black ponytail, which hung in one lengthy curl down the center of his back, seized my empty propane vessel and hooked it up to the nozzle. I waited, turned my head to the west, and it was then that I saw them.

Eyes opened wide, I stared in disbelief. In front of a bright yellow marquee with crumbling black letters was a small circular opening in the concrete that surrounded the base of the sign. Inside the space grew illustrious vines of sweet peas that flowed over the boundaries of their cement prison. It had been fifteen years since I had seen this particular flower.

I immediately walked the twenty feet it took to reach them, grabbed the stem of one flower, broke the stalk, and lifted the petals to my nose. A delicious fragrance enlivened my senses and ignited the pathways of my memory.

Suddenly, I was eleven, wearing blue shorts and a white T-shirt. My hair dangled down the middle of my back in long brown braids, my skin tanned, and my nose dotted with freckles. In front of me, a five-feet-wide plot of land boasted a harvest of budding sweet peas. My father and I had planted them a few weeks earlier on a glowing Saturday morning. He always said that this flower reminded him of me, and he even called me "sweet pea" on occasion.

I remembered that I'd kneel in the soft, brown dirt of our plot, my hands turning the soil over and over, examining for weeds. I'd grasp a weed with my fingers, clear as much dirt as possible around the root, pull it, and then place it into a pile on the grass. Afterwards, I'd pick up the accumulated discards and carry them to the garbage bins on the side of the house.

Next I'd unravel our long green hose and drag it to the flower bed, knocking over whatever flower pots lie in my path. (I was too young to be bothered with nonessentials.) A gentle spray of water would cascade from the spout, and I'd press my finger in the middle of the stream to widen its flow.

As I would water each stalk, I'd stare at the green stems that reached upward and marvel at how the tendrils knew to wrap their delicate fingers around the slender iron fence. They were bracing the entire plant for an upward climb.

In a matter of days, small buds would open, and I'd wait with anticipation to see the colors that would emerge: white, pink, red, and *deep purple*—these were my favorite. They were a rare sight in a young gardener's world. How did God make flowers the color of a plum?

On the occasional Saturday morning, my father would come outside with me to look at the flowers we had planted together, help pull the weeds, and water our tiny crop. Besides stems and petals, in that small plot of land grew a sense of ownership, and a gentle connection with my father. When my parents divorced the following year and we moved from that house, I didn't stop missing the sweet peas for years.

Suddenly, the clerk interrupted my reverie with a shout, "Ma'am, your propane is ready! Five gallons."

I looked up, said "Thank you," and resisted the impulse to wrap both of my arms around the entire lot of stems and heave my body backwards, pulling. Instead, I tucked the flower I held in the palm of my hand and folded my fingers around it. My father had been dead now for almost two years and that tiny object, to me, was so much more than just a flower. I headed back to the store, paid for the propane and set off for home.

As I drove, I thought of my father's addictions and subsequent death. The process of healing had come full circle. The passage of time had softened some of my memories and I was grateful to have remembered this one.

Now that I have finally healed, I see a renewed purpose in my life. I am here to tend the garden that the generation before me has planted, extract the weeds of the past, and reap for myself and those to follow a bountiful harvest of truth and freedom. Like a young but purposeful climber, I wrap the tendrils of my faith around strong principles and prepare myself to continue the upward venture of my progenitors.

The ability for vegetation to grow naturally is often miraculous. Despite lack of moisture, driving winds, or the cumbersome weight of soil upon it, a seed will send forth a sprout of life that instinctively knows to reach upward. Somehow, human beings possess this same innate will to live, because despite the exponential weight of life, people seem to grow and flourish beyond the burdens they carry.

I am reminded of an aunt who has buried a husband, two sons, and cares full-time for a twenty-five-year-old disabled daughter who is fully dependent upon her. My aunt is a strong, service-oriented woman with a cheerful disposition. Her days have known tragedy, but you don't see it in her eyes or hear it in her voice. Right now she is being asked to move from a home she has been living in for many years, and she is doing what she has always done—continuing the climb.

During my last trimester of pregnancy with our third son, my husband, David, was in his final semester of dental school. Caring for the two children we already had, working part-time, and growing another human being felt, at times, more than I could possibly handle. One evening as I sat on the floor folding laundry, David walked into the room and fell, completely exhausted, onto the couch.

Likewise, I turned to him, and in desperate tears exclaimed, "I cannot do this anymore. I just can't. I am too tired. I don't have anything left."

He looked at me and responded, "We don't have a choice. We have to." Though I was too tired to admit it that moment, I knew he was right. I stood up, left the laundry on the floor, and went to bed. The next morning

I rose with the renewed purpose of reaching the worthwhile destinations for which I had set out.

David's statement was precisely the right thing to say to me at the time. (However, I recommend very careful use of it with others.) If he had said, "I know, Sweetheart. If you can't do it anymore, you don't have to," I would have rolled back on the floor, lay supine, and held up the white pair of underwear I was folding as my signal of surrender.

There is a time to nurture ourselves, heal our wounds, or seek an empathetic ear. Then there is a time to stand up, tap into our driving will of survival, and just carry on with the climb. There is always more fight left in us than we realize. After a good cry or a loud scream, we remember the truth we have known before—we can keep going.

In the last few years of my father's life, I witnessed his constant struggle with depression, addiction, and personal loss. When we would speak occasionally on the phone, he would mention a determination to inch forward, no matter how slowly he was going. Until his last day, he kept his word.

He died in the middle of the night, and he was found in the morning, kneeling by his bedside in a praying position. On his desk, there was a to-do list for the next day. One of the items was to convince a neighbor that he needed to stop drinking and another was to go to church.

My life with my father reminded me very much of finding those sweet peas growing amidst the concrete in the middle of a run-down service station. They were surrounded by structural failings, but despite their environment, a beautiful garden of flowers not only bloomed, they flourished. Their very existence stated, "Take what was given to you and make it better."

Our relationship once defeated me, but having followed it through each of its stages and seeing it come full circle to healing, I now recognize its unique beauty. Despite his faults, my father offered me many values I still hold onto. He believed in God. He believed in serving others. He believed that his life had a purpose, and he looked for it everywhere.

Today I do not believe that he failed me as a parent. He just handed me the baton in the third leg of the race. His heat was done, and he would not achieve everything that he set out to on this earth. Nevertheless, he transferred into another living soul those core beliefs—God, service, and a life of purpose. Now I am here, baton of values in hand, willing to join the race, to persevere, and to reap a meaningful harvest in behalf of all of us.

"Take what was given to you and make it better" is a simple, but powerful concept. We can wither under the concrete ceilings above us, or we can grow beyond their borders. Maybe our lot in life has been difficult. So what if we didn't get everything that we planned?

We can choose to be people who forgive, who

love, who heal, and we can flower despite our surroundings. We possess an inborn will not just to live, but to be free and to live well. Just as it is innate within a flower to send its stalk toward the sun, it is innate within us to reach towards God and our highest selves, and not just survive in this life—but flourish.

Part 2

Freedom With Others

10

Life Everywhere

Indifference

IN OUR FOURTH YEAR OF MARRIAGE, MY husband, David, was accepted to dental school at the University of Pittsburgh. We were elated! We ran all of our belongings up a long, steel ramp and into the back of a moving van and headed due east. We drove across America with anticipation, but at that time, I had no idea what I'd be losing with every highway mile we gained.

David's education was costly—we could have purchased two small homes for the price of one diploma. This price tag caused me to set aside my own education so we could afford the basic needs of life. As for fringe accessories, those were impossible. Postponing my degree was the right thing to do at the time, and we planned for me to return when he finished, but the loss cut all the way through me.

Aside from my education, I lost pieces of David that I didn't recover for years. Prior to this time, he had been an active participant in our family, but he soon became a visitor in our home after 9 p.m., and occasionally on weekends. Our little family hung low on Maslow's Hierarchy of Needs, floating somewhere just above survival.

Growing up, I was the young woman ready to catch the first train out of Idaho, but when I arrived at my destination in Pittsburgh, I thought I had mistakenly been dropped off in another country. When we pulled in front of the house we were to rent on the corner of 53rd street, there were six other apartments tucked behind and above ours, all of us technically sharing one corner. It was an architectural miracle; it was architectural madness.

Our street was lined by homes thrown high in rows, each sharing a wall with a neighbor and having no yard of its own. So much was packed into so little space that we shared everything but friendship. The dilapidated commercial buildings around us begged uselessly for attention. Roof shingles scattered onto the ground, windows shamefully exposed their jagged holes, and crumbs from brick walls fell to the sidewalk like tiny morsels from a giant, dirty cake. It was obvious that no helping hands were coming to answer their cries.

Garbage lined the streets and splotches of dirt-blackened chewing gum spotted the sidewalk like ill-placed polka dots. Several times, we were awakened in the middle of the night by our neighbor's drunken boyfriend pounding on her door. In a rage, a different neighbor's ex-boyfriend threw her television and microwave out of her two-story window, claiming they both belonged to him. (Wouldn't he rather have carried them out?) One evening we were happy to see that our little community had a spot on the local news, only to find that the story was about our citizens taking back the neighborhood from the drug lords and prostitutes—a miniscule victory.

For the first few weeks, I walked around with a solid, heavy presence in my abdomen that I couldn't identify. After some time, I finally understood it. It was fear.

One morning I was getting ready to leave the house, and I noticed our neighbor outside cleaning his car. I have always prided myself on being open-minded and without prejudice, but in all my years growing up in the homogenous culture of Idaho, I had only seen a man like this in movies.

He was about six feet five inches tall, weighed approximately 280 pounds, and was an African American, with very dark skin, who looked to be in his late thirties. His neck was bigger than my entire head, with long, elaborate gold chains tumbling down from it. His fingers were decorated with enormous gold rings, and he was dressed in vibrant red and blue colored athletic clothing. He wore black sunglasses and a baseball cap.

I tried to assuage the fear that had been accompanying me since the moment we emerged from Pittsburgh's darkened Fort Pitt tunnel into the exploding city. I was going to be neighborly if it killed me, and some part of me wondered if it might. I stepped forward to speak to him.

"How are you?" I asked.

His voice bellowed forth and resonated at Grand Canyon depth as he replied, "I am blessed. I am blessed." We chatted courteously for several minutes and then went our separate ways. His name was Joe, and he was on his way to church.

I am blessed. I am blessed. Those few simple words echoed through my desperate mind. I felt anything but blessed. The careful pieces of my life were tumbling out of my control, and I was throwing a first-class party of pity, inviting anyone willing to come. As for me, I'd be sulking there indefinitely.

Joe's exclamation to me of his blessings that un-suspecting morning was the first ray of light bearing a hopeful glow in a most dreary place. I *was* a person truly blessed. I had a loving family, good health, and knowledge of God.

Despite these blessings and many others, there were certain things amiss in my mind and my heart, but discovering them turned out to be a very enlightening journey. As a human being, I had a lot of traveling to do, and over the next four years, I learned what it meant to be a distance runner.

I arrived in Pittsburgh wrapped tightly in a silk cocoon of ignorance, yet after a handful of sunsets, I crawled out of it. I lived as a nymph for a while, molting my smaller skins, and a few years later, I finally emerged into adult form. Even though I was raised in Idaho, I still claim that Pittsburgh is where I grew up.

Joe died unexpectedly of a heart attack just a few months before we moved away, and I never told him how his two words lit a candle for me at midnight. However, I am certain he knows now. In the next life, we will acutely realize the impact of our choices, large and small, and the effect they had on the people around us. Though when realization dawns, our time for love and service on the earth will have already expired.

Unfortunately, a ceiling of indifference can keep us from offering more to others. At times, we feel that the little that we have to give might not matter enough, and therefore we neglect to give it. The world of suffering and scarcity is a very big place, and unfortunately, we believe that we are very small people. Since none of us can reach everyone, everyone must be sure to reach *someone*.

If we become discouraged about what we cannot do, then we will likely withdraw our fingers from our realm, even our *right* of influence. When thousands of people withdraw their hands from others, the entire world begins to wither.

A friend once told me that after her brother died, she was sitting on her couch one afternoon, debilitated by her grief and depression. Another friend came by and dropped off a single yellow rose at the door. My friend later said, "I don't know what it was about that rose, but I got off the couch and got back to living."

Rachel Naomi Remen observed,

> *Service has a life of its own. A single act of kindness may have a long trajectory and touch those we will never meet or see. Something that we casually offer may move through a web of connection far beyond ourselves to have effects that we may have never imagined.*[14]

The divinity within us is always prompting us to serve the life around us, but we rationalize our inaction because of our busy schedules, or our own feelings of lack. Because we are each an integral part of the human race, we must agree to bear the vibrant colors of life; there is so much gray in the world that needs coloring.

Jesus Christ asked his followers to let our light "shine before men," but he never mentioned that we ought to turn the light off when no one is around, or let it dim a little when we don't think it will matter. We were asked—commanded rather—to be a light, not a light switch (Matthew 5:16).

It is unlikely that Joe intended his simple expression to give a spark of hope to a scared, young woman at the pinnacle of her fears. He was just washing his car on an ordinary Thursday afternoon. Yet the light that naturally exuded from him illuminated, for me, a tiny exit from bondage. Joe, and many others like him, reminds us of a monumental veracity of life—that we can lift the ceilings of others, simply because we carry light with us wherever we go.

11

Everyone's Hands Reach Somewhere

Insignificance

"WE CANNOT LIVE ONLY FOR OURSELVES. A thousand fibers connect us with our fellow-men; and along those fibers, as sympathetic threads, our actions run as causes, and they come back to us as effects."[15] In these few sentences, Herman Melville reminds us that we are each an integral part of a grand whole, and as we impact the world, we receive a portion of what we create.

Last week those thoughts reverberated through the chambers of my mind as two hundred pairs of eyes stared intently in my direction. My own eyes stared back at the audience, realizing just how outnumbered I was at that moment.

My name was on the program under "speaker," and I had been in a place just like this one countless times before. Yet for one passing second, I was surprised by how the people in front of me seemed to expect that I had something worthwhile to say.

The person introducing me finished and walked away from the microphone. It was my turn. I stood up, ambled forward, and turned to face my audience. I paused in silence to look into their eyes for a moment and to imagine them not as one great sea of people, but as one individual after another. I opened my mouth—and words flowed through it.

There they were.

The words I had crafted, memorized, and tucked into my cerebral hemisphere for just this occasion. I eased into the jacket of amateur orator, once again, as my entire soul remembered I actually did have something that I wanted to say.

Of course, it wasn't always like this. Seven years ago, I began my speaking career in front of a bottle of Windex. At the time, I had a two-year-old, a new baby, and a partially-finished college degree. Out of necessity, I had chosen to temporarily postpone my diploma, but I decided not to put my brain on a shelf in the meantime.

Determined to continue my education, I visited the library every week. I can still see the grimace of the librarian peering at me through her spectacles when I walked through the door. Apparently, a woman with a two-year-old and a two-month-old, both boys of the restless male variety, was not her favorite library patron.

I would stuff my backpack so full of books that I'd resort to tucking the last ones between the bottles in the diaper bag to get them all home. I soon discovered that I could wash dishes and read, make dinner and read, even do the laundry and read at the same time. When people tell me that they don't have time in their life for learning, my response is—*integrate*.

Obtaining knowledge lit a gentle fire that ran through my veins and infused my life with excitement and deeper purpose. When I was not reading, I would make up speeches about what I had learned, and then I would give presentations to dirty window panes, bottles of Windex, and rolls of paper towels, which played the part of an enduring audience.

A drive to teach others soon welled within me, and after a few months of speaking secretly in my living room, I mentioned to the youth leader in our church that I had done some speaking in the past, and I'd be interested in presenting at a youth event. Thankfully, she didn't ask the details of my experience. I doubt that a few college presentations and "speaking while vacuuming" would have been very impressive.

She called. (They do that when you offer.) She asked me to speak at a youth conference, which both terrified and thrilled me at the same time. I prepared for several weeks, and when I arrived, I peered into the room and saw 100 effervescent teenage faces that filled me with terror. My chest tightened with intimidation and my hands trembled with fear—teenagers are not the most forgiving crowd of listeners. I escaped into the restroom to look in the mirror and manufacture as much confidence as one very scared woman could fabricate. I walked out of the room and onto the stage, and I gave my presentation on living a life of high moral standards.

It was terrible.

I knew it right away. The material was incomplete, the humor wasn't funny, and the delivery lacked luster. When it was over, I sat quietly in my seat, and a very unexpected thing happened. A small, vibrant feeling of happiness took residence within me and began to swell until it finally filled me completely. A part of me was coming alive, and I knew that my small world had become bigger than just myself, even if for just one hour and even if that hour happened to be quite painful. Something inanimate, but real, was pulling me to become a spiritual teacher.

I continued to seek speaking opportunities in local church groups, mostly to the youth and women's organizations, but the next few presentations were arduous, well—terminal. Publicly, I tried to portray confidence, but a current of fear always ran below my efforts. I didn't feel I had true permission to follow such a course, and I was afraid that I'd never be good enough. Even though I worked at it, progress was slow.

It was during this time that I gave another youth workshop, and a man I knew happened to be in the audience. When it was over, I asked for his opinion and he said, "To be honest . . ."

All right, stop right there, I thought. Women know that nothing positive will follow the phrase "to be honest." Obviously, he had not been aware of the fundamental course of nature entitled "When Males Relate to Females" as he began that statement. Most women do appreciate honesty, but men must learn how to use it properly. Beginning any sentence with "to be honest" is not one of those ways. ("To be honest, you *do* look fat in those jeans. . . . To be honest, this *is* the worst meal I've ever eaten.") "To be honest," he said that my lecture wasn't very compelling, and then proceeded to tell me why.

I went home, and despite my efforts to hold them back, tears flowed freely down my cheeks and pooled onto my pillow. I lay there dejectedly. "I must be crazy. Who am I to think that I could do this?" I questioned myself.

Suddenly, a voice in my head responded, *Who are you not to?*

I wiped my eyes. Something was speaking to me and at that moment, I was ready to listen. *Why me? You always question in the back of your mind. Why* not *you? Leave your feelings of inadequacy behind you. There is a work you need to accomplish, and you will never be able to do it until you believe in it.*

I sat up and dried my eyes. *Why not me?* I had constantly feared that I wasn't good enough, but if I always agreed to feel so small, then I always would be. If I was the one who created my own feelings of inadequacy, I knew I had the power to create my own certainty.

All of me, down to the cells in my body, knew that teaching was a path I should follow. Now *that*, of course, didn't make much sense at the time. There was little evidence to support it—in fact, quite the contrary. Despite that, my belief in it could no longer be diminished. From that time on, I refused to fail.

There is a vast difference between trying hard and refusing to fail. If I reach my arm forward and *try* to pick up the glass of water in front of me, my hand might still be empty after fifteen attempts. Either I pick up the glass or I don't. Refusing to fail is to enter a deeper dimension of commitment that produces a purer quality of work.

My reading, writing, and teaching were soon transformed by the energy that exploded within me. With equal, or perhaps greater fervor, I began to ask God for help. I was human and very flawed; I had marginal knowledge and was constantly confronted by my limitations. Unless I could obtain more than what I had at the time, I'd never have anything worthwhile to offer, so I continued to bang on the doors of Heaven asking for more.

Slowly, Heaven answered. Over time, I learned how to reach deeper channels of knowledge that would grant me access when I met the conditions of vigorous study and absolute faith. I learned how to insert my whole self into what I was teaching until as a person, I disappeared completely. I discovered a better way to tell stories. I found more alluring ways to begin presentations and more memorable ways to end them. I understood when to speak and when to let silence be the teacher. I became so comfortable in front of a crowd and I had gained such a conviction of the precepts I taught that the words fell from my lips with sincerity.

Considering that public speaking is the number one fear in America—second only to death (go figure), I found many new opportunities to teach and to grow. Eventually, I started giving presentations to larger groups of people, and on one particular morning, I spoke to some Christian missionaries in Pennsylvania about self-worth. Afterwards, a woman in her sixties confessed, with tear-filled eyes, that if she had heard that message thirty years ago, her life might have been incredibly different.

Her words humbled me more deeply than any other statement possibly could, because a critical truth I had not yet fully understood suddenly became absolutely clear. This venture wasn't really about me. It included me, yes, but it was actually about God reaching other people with *His* truths. I was a tiny player in the process, but I wasn't the main character—and I never would be.

I was liberated by that fact as I intentionally began to work for God and not for myself. When I wasn't concerned about making a certain impression or even being good enough, I was free. I was free to labor for the One who had called me and to trust Him more fully. I was free to love the work and the people it included and give them the liberty to take or leave whatever they desired.

It has now been several years since I dampened my pillow one evening with defeat, and then in turn refused to be defeated. I will never forget the terrified woman whose palms once shook and voice once cracked in front of a handful of people. I keep her in a mental catalog of evidence that God can change *anyone* through His grace and power. No matter how much we lack, He can always transform us—of course, we are the ones who must knock and ask to be changed. The only thing that terrifies me more than public speaking once did is the fact that fear and self-doubt almost caused me to abandon this path. Today, besides my family, teaching means more to me than any other work I have ever pursued.

In one of his parables, Jesus Christ told the story of a group of men who were each given talents. Two of the men multiplied their talents, but the last man took the one talent that was given to him and buried it in the ground. When his day of accountability came, he declared his motivation for doing so; it was *fear* (see Matthew 25:15–29).

Each person has been given specific endowments

by our Eternal Father, and we were meant to offer these things to the world around us. If we retract ourselves because of fear, these contributions will never be presented, and the possibility of them being received is removed completely. If we have gifts but don't use them, they may just as well be buried under a giant mound of soil. However, when we claim our gifts and use them for the intended purpose of blessing the world, we glorify the Giver more than we will ever glorify ourselves.

Even though our talents were meant to bless others, our carnal presence may seek to contaminate the process. As always, the ego will attach an agenda to anything that can cause a temporary inflation of itself. When we work only for the sake of the work, or simply for the sake of others, we purify the use of our gifts. Instead of seeking a temporary ego flare—which only perpetuates our bondage in scarcity and falsehood—we create a life that is filled with deeper purpose. We then seek to become genuinely connected to others and not elevated above them.

Every contribution made on the earth was at first only a seed inside one man's mind or a dream inside of one woman's head. Once these people gave themselves permission to receive the talents they were given, they began to donate them as their own humble offerings to life. Each person has an endowment to make; this is certain. However, will every person choose to make it?

Each person holds unique gifts, and though they

may be small, they are ours and ours alone to give to the world. It is the world that we wake up in, the world where our children grow, and the world where our posterity will thrive long after we have left. Considering the vastness of the globe, the places we will go are relatively few. Yet even though we live on an enormous planet, everyone's hands reach somewhere.

I glanced up at the clock and noticed, in great surprise, that I only had five minutes left before my time was up. When I teach, the principle of time becomes absorbed by the principles of truth as my whole self becomes lost in the message.

Before I finished, I looked into the eyes of the audience one last time and remembered that what I want out of life is connected to what I am willing to bring to it.

What I want is more truth in the world, in *my* world, and for us to live in freedom from the barriers that keep us from God and our highest spiritual selves. As I make these requests, I am willing to be a part of the solution. Who am I to make such an offering?

Who am I *not* to?

12

Using Your Treasures

Materialism

LAST SUMMER I VISITED A DEAR FRIEND OF mine who I had not seen in over a year. She happened to be living at her mother's house for the summer, and I was invited to bring my three boys and stay with them for a weekend. I was overjoyed to reconnect with her, and I also felt fortunate to be in the company of her mother, who was revered as a woman who had taken the vocation of motherhood to unparalleled levels of devotion. I was eager to talk with her and learn from her experiences.

I arrived on a Sunday afternoon, and we spent the first few hours of our reunion sprawled out on the living room floor, talking excitedly. Exhausted from traveling, I grabbed a pillow from the couch to rest my head, but no sooner had the pillow touched the ground than I was informed by my friend's mother that the pillows were not allowed to leave the couch. I returned it to its place, settled for the backs of my hands, and continued on with the conversation.

That evening at dinner, I mistakenly took the "inside forks" out to the patio where the children were eating. The resident homemaker told me to put them back and directed me to take the "outside forks" instead. Later, when we watched a movie, we were allowed to eat food in the family room, but our water had to wait for us on the kitchen table. When playing on the trampoline, my boys could read stories there, but bringing popcorn or toys on its canvas was most certainly forbidden.

The next morning I wanted to make a breakfast shake, but I wasn't allowed to use the blender myself. Apparently, a mishap with an unqualified teenager ten years prior had ruined use of the blender for anyone besides the mother—*forever.* In the afternoon, I needed to do some laundry, but she would not allow me to pour the soap in myself. When I cooked dinner, I accidentally contaminated the "Atkins" chicken with my "sugary" chicken. Fortunately, the lost thirty pounds did not immediately find their way home again.

My time with my dear friend was wonderful, and as I had always been told, her mother was truly a remarkable woman who had raised children with great wisdom and dedication. Yet within a mere twenty-four hours of her company, I unintentionally ran into her iron fist everywhere I went. By the dawn of the second day, I had already crossed thirteen bylaws, and I still couldn't begin to guess what the fourteenth might be. Though nicely enforced, they were unbendable. The mother was caring and loving, yet no miniscule detail went unnoticed by her ever-attentive eyes.

After my boys were chastised because they climbed the "apple" tree instead of the "ash" tree, I was ready to forfeit my guest room. With all the love in the world and some chocolates purchased by the hostess especially for me, I stepped out the door with my luggage in hand and looked down at my feet. They rested on a mat that said, "Welcome."

It stands to reason that most of us value our possessions because we have worked hard for what we've acquired. My weekend stay reminded me, however, that one of the most important ways we can treasure our things is by allowing them to be used.

I once knew a man who said that he valued books so much he'd only buy them brand new and in hardback. The select ones that had been read were each outlined in the same color and format and displayed neatly on a bookcase with museum-like perfection.

As a treasurer of books, I am also quite careful

about how I use them. I usually purchase them already used to increase my buying capacity, and in paperback, because they bend well into purses, backpacks, and my swimming tote. A paperback folded right down the center fits perfectly under the front seat of our truck.

I'm willing to grab any writing utensil I can find to mark a passage including (but not limited to) a pen borrowed from a waitress, colored pencils from the floor in church, scrapbook markers, children's crayons, and in desperation, an eyeliner pencil has scribbled illegibly onto a page or two.

Our family treasures books by using them and using them everywhere. Doctor's waiting rooms have sheltered me while I squeezed out the last drops of insight from pages I couldn't leave. We take children's books to restaurants and parks or read them aloud when traveling in the car. If a public lecturer is holding us hostage with boredom, we always have a spare book for retreat.

One of my books still carries a few cinders from a campfire in northern Arizona, and others have blades of grass from the fields of Pennsylvania. Some books carry movie tickets, napkins from restaurants, or homemade paper airplanes, revealing secrets of where they've been to those who next open their pages.

We use them, we lend them out, we borrow them, and at times, we lose them. Occasionally, we have to buy them again. Considering the profits we reap from the luxury of verbal lexis, it's a very small price to pay. We are wealthy because we gather their diamonds and take them with us.

If we treasure our possessions, we should remember that we decidedly increase their value every time we use them. I have been in homes you cannot live in, on carpet you should not walk on, and in clothing that I was afraid to hold a small child while wearing. Of course, it is important for us to take care of the things we own and to teach our children to do the same, but we must remember that the primary purpose of our things is to serve *us*, and not for us to serve them. Enlightened people can find a good balance.

Excessive love of material possessions is a ceiling, a dead ceiling of dead things, which can hinder authentic happiness. If we are too attached to our things, we are more likely to sacrifice the living people in our lives for the accumulation of inanimate objects. For example, many parents feel that they must have fine things for their children—only to be forced to leave those children to work long hours to serve the things in their lives more than the people.

Millions of people spend either more money than they make or the exact equivalent of their earnings. By choice, they become fenced in by financial bondage, which takes them prisoner. They *must* have the things that money can buy them, even if it costs them their personal relationships, improved health, or a peaceful mind. They are enslaved to a system that believes that the sum of material goods can somehow increase the sum of personal value, but as history has already proven, slavery can only be upheld by falsehood.

Our carnal presence will always tempt us to attach personal meaning to our material things, because it fears there is not enough meaning in who we are without them. Our home is not just a place where we reside together; the ego uses it to measure status. The vehicle is not what drives us around; it is used for a personal statement. The clothes are not for covering our body; they are used to show it off. However, our spirit—our true identity—has never needed temporary possessions to enhance its eternal reality.

All physical things are in a state of deterioration. Every tree will decompose, every sheet of steel will rust, every brick will crumble, and every piece of fabric will eventually disintegrate. Security cannot be found in what is passing. We must choose to let die what is already dying before we can truly grasp what lives and has no end. In this realm, we find freedom from carnal hunger, the hunger of the ego, which no amount of material goods can ever adequately fill.

An authentic life of freedom requires that we relinquish our dependence on the trappings of the physical world. We can use material possessions for the narrow purpose of their creation, without becoming human subjects to inanimate masters. These masters are empty of real meaning, with no power to love us or to save us from the insecurity we carry. Why is it that we love them so fiercely?

Eventually, all of my books will be passed on, but their truths will be tucked within me. All of our clothes will be given away, but the memories we made while wearing them will remain. The house will be sold, but the love between the people who lived there will still flourish.

In the end, we will keep nothing we can touch with our fingers. All we have is who we are, which stands separately from everything we have owned. If we exist in bondage to the physical world, our inner life will wither. Yet when we declare our freedom from the material realm, we become wise and masterful stewards of the physical sphere, but more importantly, the eternal.

13

Keeping Your Limbs

Social Conformity

DURING A RECENT VISIT TO A SHOPPING mall, I almost wondered if an important part of womanhood had somehow overlooked me. I was buying a bra at a store that claims to fit "any size," but after a few unsuccessful minutes in the fitting room, the sales clerk suggested that I might have better luck in the teen department at Nordstrom's.

Well, then. I picked my surprise up off the floor, attached it to my chest in the place where different breasts apparently should have been, and stood a little taller. "Thanks for your help," I said, and fortunately, I walked out with my confidence in tact. That experience confirmed, in yet another way, the fact that I am not an ordinary woman. Thankfully for my ego, I've relinquished my desire to be one.

I first faced this truth while we were living in the eastern United States. It was quickly pointed out to me that I was the youngest mother in my son's kindergarten class, and I also happened to have the most children, both socially uncommon practices in our region of the country. People questioned aloud if I was the mother or the baby-sitter. (I've been up since 4:00 a.m.—I am most certainly the *mother*.)

With certain types of people, it seems that I would fit into my surroundings better if I were willing to chop off one or two of the arms that make up my being. Yet time and time again, I am forced to choose in favor of my limbs. If you have ever lost important parts of yourself to the blades of social amputation, you know the freedom of settling back into your own skin and wearing it around unabashedly.

As a country, we are an eclectic mix of national-ity, race, and religion, yet somehow we feel pressure to fit our lives into the small parameters of our social neigh-borhood. Diversity may be on some political agendas, but uniformity is the unwritten rule that governs our communities where being different is not a privilege; it's almost a burden.

I am reminded of a friend of mine who told me that when her mother was pregnant she owned two maternity dresses, one red and one black. While wearing the red one, a woman at church remarked that a pregnant woman dressed in red resembles a barn on a farmyard. Now her mother has only one maternity dress.

Do we not realize how much we lose when we try to shove people, who are very spacious beings, into the infinitesimal niches of popular opinion? On our birth certificates, some of us would do well to have a line of permission included that states "Be who you are and do so anywhere." Just as the most alluring rivers crawl their own careful way to find the ocean, the most intriguing people are the ones who create their own paths and make no apologies for stepping off society's well-traveled highways.

At times, we feel that we must secure permission to be who we really are, to think what we really think, and to choose the path that we know is right for us. However, we already acquired that freedom at birth, and as we came forth naked and screaming into the world, we exuded the raw reality of our power of choice.

Unfortunately, many of us have forgotten that truth, and we are in need of reclaiming it. In *Give Me Liberty*, Gerry Spence writes:

> *We give permission for (others) to enslave us when we take their judgments of us as our own. When the teacher tells the child her drawing does not look like a tree, when the psychologist tells the person he is abnormal . . . when we are told that our most passionate goals are impossible, or our most heartfelt longings stupid, when*

we are compared to others as not measuring up—these judgments (are) foisted upon us daily . . . By what right do they judge us? By what authority? **They judge us by the authority we have given them to judge us.** *We cannot prevent their judgments, but their judgments are as useless as ciphers unless we accept them as legitimate for us.*[16] *(Emphasis added by this author.)*

The expectant mother in the red dress was not belittled into a diminished wardrobe by another person. She *agreed* to it. If she hadn't agreed, she'd still be wearing crimson with a smile.

If we have been stifled and trapped under a ceiling of social anxiety, we ought to remember that freedom is found through the skylight of our own permission. Only then can we reach the enlightened gulf of our own true personage.

That is the life of a friend of mine who faithfully home schools five children, though she has received constant interrogation about not choosing the normal way of education. However, isn't "social norm" what some of us fear the most? She chooses in favor of her own best judgment, rather than in favor of the crowds.

Of course, we must always take caution not to use "personal choice" as a rationale from stepping away from eternal truth, which unfortunately is a widespread phenomenon in our world today. Instead, we ought to use it as a reason to propel us *toward* truth.

The more I learn, the more I feel it is necessary to break certain social agreements in order to pursue higher paths. I cannot choose in favor of fitting in or being liked if it causes me to sacrifice my path towards God.

Our world pays regular and expensive homage to falsehood. Far too many of us agree to espouse our lives to false theories rather than carefully dissect the difference between fact and fiction. For example, many families work desperately to get ahead, when they really should be working desperately to get *together*—and stay that way. For many people, family solidarity has been sacrificed for a higher climb on the ladder of monetary status. Nevertheless, families need security, deep roots, and time with each member more than they need expensive vacations and new vehicles.

Furthermore, our culture asks women to bare our bodies to reveal the full measure of our beauty. Yet the world is in desperate need of women who will bare greater wisdom, deeper character, and heightened spirituality. Popular culture assigns value to what is seen and measured in women, rather than what is unseen, but infinitely valuable. Many women have become lost in the tide of opinion as they become washed out and used up by an enigmatic social entity that has no ability to assess their true, eternal value.

Wayne Dyer states,

> When you stay plugged into group consciousness, you are really saying, 'I choose to evolve slowly.' Furthermore, the mind-set always gives you permission to be weak

and impotent. You choose to evolve with a group rather
than spontaneously, as your inner conscious dictates.[17]

"Group consciousness" is a lethargic entity, and we must not consign ourselves to evolve at its sleepy speed. There are social rules of conformity that we must break in order to keep higher principles of truth, because ultimately, the unconscious world around us is not responsible for our freedom—we are. The people we know and their opinions are not responsible for our choices—we are. The power of choosing our own path cannot be taken away from us. If we don't retain full responsibility for our choices, it is only because we have given that responsibility away to a source other than ourselves.

There may always be loyalists to popular culture. There will always be those who cling to the well-trodden paths of social inclusion for the comfort of the huddled masses. Yet to the red maternity dress wearers, the women buying bras in teenage stores, and every human river crawling its own way through societal paths to seek higher ground—the only permission we have ever needed is our own.

14

Play Land

Over-Seriousness

WAITING FOR YOUR KIDS TO EMERGE FROM the play structure at a fast-food restaurant is like waiting for a space ship to land. By the time the child puts his feet back down on the ground, his hair has grown shoulder length, and he speaks a second language.

I used to wonder why my youngest son didn't at least come down to eat, but I soon understood when he toddled out with a cheeseburger that *I* hadn't given him. Thankfully, the facility has adapted to my concerns—I recently had a server ask me if I would like immunizations with our Happy Meals. Regular or supersize?

I have seen Haley's comet pass more often than I've seen a child bomb down that red slide and willingly put on his shoes. Is it a ploy from restaurant executives? They know your recently expanded childbearing hips are not going to fit up that little purple tunnel to retrieve them. If they can keep you there a few months longer, when your children finally materialize, they'll be ravenous for a Big Kids' Meal, which strategically costs more than the kiddie size.

All over the globe, even health conscious, germ-enlightened mothers have decided to forfeit to the culture of the golden arches. We have realized that a childhood without a dose or two of fast food and all its amenities may procure an uncommon attachment to it later in life. How do you think those teenagers inhaling fried chunks of processed chicken ended up in the ball area? Just last week, I asked a sixteen-year-old young man to stop sliding down the spiral slide on his serving tray while my two-year-old played at the bottom. He questioned defiantly, "Why? I'm not hurting anyone."

I'm writing this chapter while sitting on a bright yellow bench. Next to me is a plastic fish toy that is the designated must-have for those five and under. I am waiting for my children to remember that they came with a mother, and that as the years pass, they might actually want to find her.

Oh, I think I see one. I'm not sure, but he looks a little like his father did at age twelve. He walks up to me, now with braces, and asks for a Big Kids' meal in

French. All right, leaders of the fast food universe—you win—and I pull out my wallet.

"Order it for me, Mom, I'll be right back," he shouts as he bounds up an electric blue slide and disappears.

For another decade.

I have been reminded countless times that whole sections of life cannot be survived without our willingness to laugh. Some say laughter is the best medicine, but often laughter is our only option. I am certain that God has a sense of humor; otherwise, He would not have made many of us. (Those of you that are thinking of your neighbors—that's not nice.)

Taking ourselves and our lives too seriously accumulates a ceiling of clouds that will rain unhappiness down upon our drooping heads. However, if we look closely, an undercurrent of humor runs just below the grave rivers of human existence. Tapping into it exposes a critical lifeline to survival, especially in parenting. We can talk about solutions or draft resolutions in stone, but only a good hearty laugh can save the day when you enter the backyard and your four-year-old and his friend are running around naked pretending to smoke cigarettes— and his mother is following behind you.

I am reminded of the night I was lying on my son's bed waiting for him to return from the bathroom so that we could read a bedtime story. He walked into

the room with an enormous pitcher of water being carefully balanced in both hands, stepping slowly. When he
reached me, he lowered his head to take a sip. I opened
my mouth to ask him to put it back in the kitchen, when
he smiled mischievously, bounded forward, and dumped
half of its contents on me.

I'm sure the planning stages of his practical
joke seemed harmless as the rushing water began to
pool at the bottom of his pitcher—even during the fake
sip he did not anticipate the consequence of his prank.
However, after seeing his entire bed saturated along with
the mother who was in it, he stared at me with fear and
wonder. And I stared back at him with fear and wonder.
How does a six-year-old craft this kind of bravery?

This happened to be one time that I paused
long enough to contemplate my options before choosing the nearest response from the motherhood shelf.
Unfortunately, my silence caused him to take courage.
Though his body remained completely still and his face
expressionless, he flung his arms forward and threw the
rest of the water on me. My hair was drenched. Beads of
water dripped down my face, carrying my makeup with
them.

Again he stared at me, without a smile, searching
for my reaction. I lay there stunned. The pitcher had only
a few drops to spare, and the deed was done. I was already
wet, as was his bed and all of his bedding.

I opened my mouth wide, looked right into his

eyes, threw my head back, and laughed. He finally exhaled the laugh he had been holding for eternity. I laughed even harder.

"But if you ever do that again, we'll sell you to the zoo." He never has, and we're both still laughing.

When we're drowning in seriousness, humor is a flotation device that can save us when nothing else can. It saved me when I walked into the kitchen and found two dozen cherry tomatoes splattered all over the ceiling, the walls, and the floor. I was informed there had been a pitching contest for speed.

Humor can save you when the baby-sitter runs into a wall, is knocked out cold, and your children, plus three boys from the neighborhood, have a contest shooting pinto beans through straws in your living room.[18] And after some carefully contrived discipline, humor can privately restore your sanity when your children tie a different baby-sitter to a chair and throw all of their clothing out the second story window. It's a wonder that baby-sitters work for so little money.

Many of our life experiences will be hilarious in twenty years. We can laugh or cry now, but we're certain to be laughing later, so we might as well enjoy them early. Great emphasis is put on "survival of the fittest," but sometimes being fit to survive is a willingness to be entertained by the life that could just as easily run you over. When frustration, embarrassment, or aggravation construct an atmosphere that threatens to smother us, humor can at least keep a window open.

Our family recently went to see a movie and walked into the darkened theater just as it was starting. With limited seating available, my husband escorted the oldest boys to the front row and I hovered in the back with the baby. I finally found one seat open in the handicap aisle, which was perfect for the stroller I was carting. We sat down, and seconds later, I heard a man shouting at another person behind me.

"*You're blah, blah, blah . . .*" I couldn't make out what he was saying, but it was clear that he was angry.

A few seconds later, I heard him again. "*You're sitting . . . blah, blah!*" I still could not understand him, but now he was really making a commotion. Several people turned around, including me.

This time he screamed loud enough for most of the theater to hear, "*You are sitting in my wheelchair!*" I looked up at him. I looked down at my seat.

I was sitting in a wheelchair.

Why I didn't notice right away and why he, himself, wasn't using it, I don't really know. However, I do know that when a sea of people stares our way, we have to find that lifeline of humor, grab hold with both hands, and never let go. We may not survive life without it.

15

Laying Down the Gavel

Judgment

NESTLED NEAR THE BANKS OF THE SNAKE River in Idaho Falls, Idaho, is a one-story home with white siding and a single car garage directly attached to the west wall. In front of the house is a weeping willow tree that ascends thirty feet high into the air with branches that drape down to the ground in dramatic, sweeping arches.

If you visited there today, it is likely that an old car in ill condition, waiting to be restored, is parked on the side of the house. Below the living room window, there are brittle remains of wild flowers that once sprouted forth blossoms in their fertile beds, but now bend to the earth as evidence that their short life was choked by dehydration.

The corners of the cement stairs leading up to the porch have crumbled away—the result of a young boy who wielded a hammer many years ago, wondering how long it would take to break apart concrete one strike at a time. Upon entering the house, you would hear the penetrable squeak of the front door that fails to latch, swinging open at the will of the breeze.

In the living room, you would see one hundred sheets of Bach music glued to the wall, posing as wallpaper behind the piano. In that same room, between two stiff lounge chairs, you might hear the sound of a parakeet screeching an inharmonious song.

In the kitchen, you would immediately discover that the cupboards held no doors, revealing their entire contents at one inspecting glance. In the bathroom, you would recognize that instead of a shower head, a pipe protrudes out of the wall, spitting forth just enough water to make a weary bath.

You might possibly find last night's meal dried in a pan on the stove, last month's mail piled high onto the kitchen table, and last year's laundry dumped onto the stairs, trickling down to the cement floor of the basement. Of course, the most intriguing part of the house is the backyard, but if you dare to enter, be careful not to get pecked by the goose, bitten by the goat, slimed by the duck, or inspected by the resident chinchilla.

Walking on the Ceiling

If you walked through this home, you may cast a judgment or two—or three, but those initial thoughts would never reveal the truth of the woman who lives here. If you judged first, thus constricting your mind, you'd miss one of the priceless treasures that this neighborhood, even this city built around a river has to offer.

Most of these oddities have come to pass at the hands of Val, the occupant homemaker. She is a home improvement activist that eagerly begins new projects and considers it good timing if she finishes in five years.

The reason the front door doesn't latch is because it maintains an open corridor for any weary traveler, any lost animal, any unwed mother, any mentally ill patient, or any child in need of a home—whether temporary or permanent. When most doors slam shut, this one still swings open.

Val may leave home projects unfinished for years, but she completes human beings with a love unparalleled by others. It doesn't matter who you are, where you have been, or what you have done wrong, she can love you.

As a teenager, she hired me to assist her in home projects. In fact, I was the one who glued sheets of Bach's concertos to the living room wall. Aside from learning how to plumb a toilet and hammer out sections of sheet rock to build introverted book shelves (I'm fierce with a table saw), she taught me to look beyond what you know *about* people and see the real person.

She paid me hourly to help her, but as an unsure

structure myself, I was the one in need of home improvement. I used to wonder, *I am such a wreck. How can she not see it?* Later, I realized that she did see it. However, she saw also beyond it. One night as we talked on her degenerating front steps she said, "I'll always keep the bed made in the back room just for you."

I never did end up sleeping on that bed, but I knew with certainty that this woman loved me dearly for no reason at all. There was nothing I had done to earn it. I had nothing to offer her in return, but she loved me freely. In her company, I felt that I was more worthwhile than I had ever before suspected.

There are some impressions that never leave you.

If a person were to look around a room and pick up any familiar object, she would claim to know that particular thing. For example, if I were to pick up the pencil sitting on my desk right now, I would say with certainty that I know what that object is, but how do I know this?

I know it from past experience. I have written with pencils before, sharpened them, and thrown one away when it was too short. The reason that I know the pencil in front of me is because I bring all prior knowledge of pencils with me when I see it. That same phenomenon occurs when we assess other objects around us. We feel that we know them right now, because we have known them previously.

This particular process helps us adapt quickly and function effectively in our world. By carrying previous information with us, we do not have to reassess the purpose of the items around us each time we see them. This is an efficient tool when it comes to objects; however, it is incredibly damaging when it comes to people. When we apply this process into our relationships, we suffer from the illusive belief that we know people. In actuality, this practice keeps us from knowing them at all.

Several years ago, I was riding a bus in Ocean City, Maryland, while on vacation. At one of the stops, a young man with an unforgettable appearance sat down directly in front of me. He had jet black hair, a black T-shirt, several nose and lip rings, and large silver-studded jewelry adorning his neck and wrists. I found his speech and his behavior to be disrespectful and quite offensive. My first thoughts were those of judgment—I had known people like this before. Then another thought came, *You don't know him at all.*

I pondered that truth on the drive back to my hotel. It was true; I didn't know him. Where did he live? What was his mother's name? What was his childhood like? What were his biggest fears? Was he close to his father? What dreams did he have for his future? God had created him, just as He had created me, and I wondered if this young man even knew that. The arrogant belief that I knew people "like this" was the very ceiling that kept me from knowing him at all.

When my stop finally came and I walked past him to the exit, I was filled with compassion toward him, and I had the sudden urge to throw my arms around his iron-clad neck. (I doubt his friends would have thought that was very cool.) I resisted the impulse. However, when I stepped onto the sidewalk, I understood how it is possible to be looking right at people and never actually see them. How many thousands of people in my life had I stared at, while completely blind?

How judgment effects the mind is similar to how cholesterol affects an artery. As judgment collects, it creates a blockage for positive connections to flow freely between two people. Judgment constricts us—our minds and our emotions—as we interact with each other. In *Wherever You Go, There You Are*, Jon Kabbatt-Zin teaches:

> *While our thinking colors all our experience, more often than not our thoughts tend to be less than completely accurate. Usually they are merely uninformed private opinions, reactions and prejudices based on limited knowledge and influenced primarily by our past conditioning . . . We get caught up in thinking we know what we are seeing and feeling, and in projecting our judgments out onto everything we see off a hairline trigger.*[19]

It is not until we become the watchful observers of our minds that we realize we are active, even overactive, participants in this damaging process. Imagine a trip to the park. You notice that it is a little windy, and your mind makes a judgment that this is bad. Nevertheless, the sun is shining (good). Your friend is late (rude). A woman is angry with her kids (bad mother). One person's shirt doesn't match her shorts (careless). There is some garbage on the ground (trashy). A father reads while his kids play (distant parent). As we begin to pay careful attention, especially in social situations, we will witness our minds taking in information, and immediately attaching a label to it.

Our judgments are an autonomic reaction to the experiences, teachings, opinions, and perceptions that we have culminated throughout the years. It can be difficult to recognize a phenomenon that has camouflaged itself into the landscape of our paradigm. For example, many people live with an ingrained prejudice against certain religions, particular occupations, specific areas of the city they live in, a particular brand name of clothing, or even a certain automobile manufacturer. Thousands of judgments may live within us and operate beyond our recognition.

Judgment is a learned behavior. Young children do not exhibit judgment until adults teach it to them. Fortunately, if the behavior is learned, then it can be unlearned. We can retrain our minds by watching closely as each judgment enters our thoughts. When we notice one, we simply choose to remain unattached to its message—meaning that we do not take it for the truth. Over time, we realize that most of our thoughts represent patterns of mental conditioning, not actual reality. This practice of observation causes a separation to occur between our perception and the damaging thought. In a sense, we are watching the thought and therefore, we are not controlled by it.

Social situations are useful practice sessions where we can pay careful attention to the judgmental thoughts that arise in our minds. In times of practice, I have nodded in recognition at each judgment, and have even counted them to maintain alert observation. After judgment # 17, this habit becomes almost humorous. We realize how often uninvited thoughts of judgment enter our minds, but because we are not influenced by their messages, we are free of their potentially damaging influence.

Many years ago, when our family moved into a new neighborhood and we began interacting in our community, my mind would automatically seek to dissect people according to the bits and pieces of information we learned about them. However, when I focused on opening myself and my mind simply to *receive* other people, I began to feel a genuine connection to them, despite any physical differences that may have existed between us.

If we ask ourselves, "What would we be like if our minds were clear of judgment?" The answer would be—*free*. We would open ourselves to others and not live as isolated beings behind walls of separation that we have crafted one harmful thought at a time.

Judgment constricts us—it narrows our minds and reinforces an ever-present boundary we impose on human relations. However, other people rarely suffer from our judgments as much as we do. We feel the constriction that usually causes tension within us. We feel the isolation that comes from cutting ourselves off from others. Simply stated, we lose the benefit of being connected to each member of the human family without reservation.

We are in grave need of preserving open connections with each other. Today countries war with other countries, neighbors hate their neighbors, friends despise old friends, and families sever from each other, never to reunite again.

The connection we need to maintain with the people around us, as well as with the whole human race, is only possible when we change the mental screen through which we view the world. When we change the way we think, we will change the way we feel. When we change the way we feel, we will change the way we live. When we change the way we live, we will lay down the gavel.

And we could all use a little mercy.

16

Where You're Planted

The Past

TWELVE WEEKS AFTER I GRADUATED FROM high school in southern Idaho, I prepared to leave my hometown. After the last pair of shoes had been shoved inside of a brand new suitcase and a final box of laundry soap was stuffed into the trunk of the car, I stuck a mental Post-it note on our front door, stating that I would not be coming back. *Ever.*

It took me ten years to take that note down.

I always believed that I was a seedling planted in Idaho, without my permission. When I was twelve, I told my friends that I wanted to live in central Africa, where I'd dig irrigation ditches and make clothing for the

Congolese children. When I was a teenager, I imagined a life in the Peace Corp. I'd live in the Middle East, caring for hundreds of orphans while nursing young male rebels back to health in my spare time. Our small city just didn't throw enough sparks to flame my aspirations for adventure.

Growing up, when my fellow teenage comrades would mention to adults that Idaho was a boring place to live, we would inevitably hear the reply, "Only the boring get bored." However, the city of Rigby—fifteen minutes from where I grew up—was rumored to have the most teenage pregnancies per capita in the nation. Teenagers have a way of easing boredom, with or without parental consent.

After hanging onto Idaho's fringes for a few years, I finally left for good with plenty of wind behind my young sails. When we relocated to Pennsylvania, the most attention my home state received from me was when I corrected the topographically challenged by explaining that my state of origin was not "Iowa."

"Did you live on a potato farm?" was their next question.

"No, but rogue potatoes in transport occasionally hit my windshield." They laughed because they thought I was making a joke. Little did they know that many Idahoan schools still release their students for a weeklong period called "Spud Harvest," and dances and community picnics are constructed around this festivity.

In fact, one of my high school romances ensued after one such "Harvest Ball." (Love ignites easily while wearing matching plaid flannel.) Most people do not comprehend that the real treasure of the Gem State has never been a precious stone. It has always been, and may forever be...a potato.

After my East Coast relocation, I did return home once a year for a visit, but just long enough to cast a furtive glance at those who ate roast beef every Sunday evening for twenty years in a row. As a more cultured adult, I even began to pronounce the "ing" at the end of my words. "I oughta get goin'" was just somethin' I wasn't gonna say anymore. I was grateful to have finally gathered my roots and transplanted them into the bigger cities and wider circles that were now before me. After each visit, I gave that Post-it note a sporadic press, some extra Scotch tape, and set it firmly in place—behind me.

It took one marriage, three children, four moves, five jobs, and ten years before I returned to crack open the doors I had sealed in such haste. A high school reunion had fallen into my lap, and I knew I needed to return home for more than one reason. I was a new species since I left Idaho—same brown hair but different heart—and there was a disparate section of my life that needed to be reclaimed.

Many seasons had come and passed in my life. I left home in the wild optimism of summer, but I only survived by endless work in the autumn, amidst trials that aged my ignorance. The stifling winds of previous winters changed me into one who sought grace instead of censure. Now it was spring again, and along with the rest of nature, I had opened myself to all of life.

This reunion was perfect timing. High school is one life experience from which most of us need to recover. It's just the age when we begin to develop our self-concept, but it's a harsh initiation. We want to know who we are, but we allow everyone else to tell us. When the sum of your worth hinges on brand name clothing or a cheerleading mini-skirt—neither of which happened for me—your self-esteem can't help but be jumbled.

Even the studs in letterman jackets who floated on the sheer air of popularity (most often above *me*) had to touch the ground after graduation. A mean dunk shot doesn't get you a raise in the business world, and in marriage, "hard to get" only gets you a night on the couch.

Ten years had done wonders for my own self-concept, which had recovered from never being crowned homecoming queen. Besides that, I needed to confront a gentleman named Jack, who stuck his finger down his throat to gag himself when I asked him to dance in the seventh grade. I was over it, but he still needed some chastisement.

So off I drove from my new home in the desert back to the mountains of my origin. As my headlights devoured the white lines of the highway, my mind dissolved the gray lines of the past—and an awakening occurred.

My mental Post-it note, once so firmly in place, had been carried away by the breeze of a new discovery. I realized that no matter what course I had traveled, the only time I had was the present time. Ancient judgments could dissolve in the conscious awareness of the single day that I lived in, and my old state of mind didn't have to contaminate a new field of awareness. I was no longer running from my roots, nor making up for them; I was just awake and alive one current moment at a time.

As I crossed the state line, I was fully present for the journey. I ascended the rise of one mountainside and was stopped breathless at the view that unspooled before me. Indigo and cerulean hues loomed above, frosted by the residence of still-white snow. The mountains were bathed in a hundred shades of green life, adorned by billowing clouds hanging above.

I opened my window to smell air so crisp that I was afraid to inhale too deeply, lest it should dissipate. I had forgotten to miss that until now. It was the first door I opened on that soil, but it would not be the last.

Over the coming days, I cracked open many old padlocks. I opened the door to my mother and found her to be loving, stalwart, and far more wonderful than I had previously understood. I opened the door to my grandparents, and I discovered the wealth of my heritage. I opened the door to my hometown, and found it was lush and rich with flavor. These rooms of my past had not really changed since I left; I had opened.

I finally pulled into the parking lot of the Shilo Inn. The famous locale of our high school dances was hosting yet another homecoming. When I first walked in the doors, my eyes fell upon an attractive man, and it took me a moment to recognize him. A decade prior he had been overweight with pale, ruddy skin, no facial hair, and severe acne. All of this had reversed, and his self-concept had adjusted as well.

I talked with another person who was a class clown in high school, but was now an emergency room doctor. (Yet after hearing some of his stories, I made a note never to become sick, maimed, or injured if I were ever in Missouri.) Jack, absent because of rumored delinquent behavior, did not get that talk that he had coming. In addition, one of those floating-on-air jocks with his feet now on the ground stumbled to his feet to envelop my hand and engage me in conversation.

The universe had finally come into balance.

When we start new chapters in our lives, we have a tendency to shut our old history books when we don't find what we are looking for within their pages. We likely assume that what we desire is somewhere further down the road. Without inner transformation, slick fingers from the grave slide around our throats, and we cannot move forward because we are in bondage to the very past we're running from. Prior marriages, old jobs, previous mistakes, or failed relationships act as ceilings that block our progress. Unless we heal from the past, we are prone to recreate it.

The only place freedom is achieved is in the small space of *now*. We become free when our current self has expanded beyond what we once struggled with—when we choose to forgive the people from our past instead of continuing to blame them or when we desire peace for others instead of ill-will. In reality, the past no longer exists. It only survives as a mental construction that we access in the present. Yet without personal transformation in the here and now, we will always bring our old selves with us, and thus recreate a new version of an old bondage.

"Bloom where you are planted" is a line that I often saw cross-stitched and toll-painted in Idahoan homes. I once chuckled at the craft, but now I am astounded at the wisdom. We can sink our personal roots in whatever soil we find below our feet and our freedom will flower to the height that we are grounded in truth and peace at the present time. This is when we no longer run from the past; we make friends with it.

My revolutionary trip to Idaho lasted two weeks. Then it was time to leave. I loaded my suitcases into the truck and drove off in a wake of quaking aspens, weeping birch trees, and the bidding arms of my family, who had graciously wrapped their love around me.

Round, full bushes of sage swayed at the wind of

my tires. I drove through the stillness of the mountains just as the sun blushed the top of each crest, and I drew in one more deep breath of fresh Rocky Mountain air. I already missed my mother. I was leaving home once again, but I was glad I left that Post-it note on the door.

This time it read "I'll be back."

17

Down From the Mountain

Self-Righteousness

AS AN ASPIRING AUTHOR, I ONCE GREW frustrated at the household tasks that pulled me away from my passion of writing. After addressing twelve loads of laundry, cluttered closets, and dirty dishes, I was surprised that I could sit down at my desk, put two fingers on my wrist and still locate a creative pulse.

However, I soon realized that if I dismissed myself from my life too long, my writing would become old and stale like the end pieces of a loaf of bread I had forgotten to throw away. I quickly learned that it was *living* that enhanced my writing by providing vivid detail, live material, and an animated backdrop for the paragraphs.

As much as I'd like to lock myself in the basement with only a computer and a small trap door for food, it is the details of my life that breathe vibrancy onto my pages, so they can be created in full color instead of dull variations of gray. I mistakenly believed that withdrawing from my life would allow me to become better at my work, yet the opposite was true. It was in life's presence, not its absence, where I drew closer to what I was seeking.

I find this to be equally true when it comes to inner transformation. Just after we have climbed a high spiritual mountain, we sometimes find it difficult to come back to our old habitat again. In the absence of that life, it was easy to feel "transformed." We supposed that we had catapulted ourselves to the sky in understanding, but when our feet touched back down on the earth, at times we became frustrated with the people who were the same as when we left them.

Yet this frustration with others becomes its own boundary, a hidden one that spontaneously emerges just when we thought we were getting somewhere on the path of freedom. We may authentically seek God, love, peace, and truth, but our condescension for those who do not value those things pulls us further away from the changes we're after.

Occasionally, we choose to retreat to seclusion for safety. There are exclusive times, with certain people, in which that might be necessary. However, the sky isn't where we really become exalted. It is in the presence of our life, not its absence, where we find the lasting transformation we desire.

As spiritual seekers, we soon become aware that there is a space between our principles and our practice— a gap between what we know is true and then how we live that truth. Increasing our knowledge while immersed in spiritual teachings is critical; however, it is in the details of our lives where it becomes regular practice.

For example, I once listened to someone teach about forgiveness and within ten minutes, I became completely devoted to the concept. Of course, it then took me several years to fully transfer the mental idea into heartfelt action. A friend of mine once told me that he would have a great day at work as a spiritual teacher, and on the drive home, he would make a commitment to be loving and patient with his family when he arrived. However, three minutes after walking through the door, he would become agitated and critical towards them. After discussing the matter one day, I suggested in jest that he walk in the house, announce his profound love to his family, and then go quickly up to his bedroom to be alone.

There are certain books I have ingested that have revolutionized my way of thinking, and I've wanted to immerse myself in their pages again and again. It seemed that if I could only steal a few more minutes of solitude from my busy life, surely I'd achieve enlightenment right there on the living room couch. That is probably as likely as someone reading about baseball long enough and being drafted to the starting lineup in the major league without ever playing the game. You don't learn spirituality on the couch, but in the field of life. That is where cognitive knowledge becomes experiential knowledge—when we take the words off the page and breathe them into the finite workings of our daily living.

Of course, we should continue a voracious search for information and sink up to our waistlines in true principle, but after we've learned something celestial, we need to carry it with us. We are going to need it when the frustrated child walks in the door, we're at the office, or the neighbor sues us.

Last week, I had an experience that reminded me of the importance of practicing our principles. I was on my way to a department store to do some shopping, and prior to leaving, I spent a very meaningful hour of prayer, meditation, and reading. On the drive there, I rehearsed a spiritual lesson I was due to give the following weekend and the morning had been very tranquil and enriching.

Upon arrival, I crossed one of the aisles and noticed an elderly woman sitting on a bench crocheting. I turned my head, gave her a friendly smile, and at the same moment, she spoke to me.

"Life sucks, doesn't it, Honey?" she said loudly, dropping a bomb of negativity on my morning of euphoria.

Taken back in surprise, I still managed a smile

and a response, "Well, actually, I think it's pretty great most of the time."

She jeered at me. "That's because you're young!"

"Well, when I'm older, I hope I still feel that way," I responded with my smile fading a bit and my condescension heightening a little.

"You won't," she sneered. "You're young, and you don't have any bad kids yet!"

I could see that this was counter-productive, so I chose to abandon the small ship of space we shared with a smile and a short, "Have a nice day."

As I walked away, she shouted at me, "You're young, Honey! You're young!"

I continued to walk down the aisles. Along with a new pair of pants, I realized that I was carrying some fresh contention with me. When I noticed it, I asked for forgiveness. What good is an hour of spiritual solitude in the morning when I can't spend five minutes in peaceful communion with another human being? Even if that love is not returned, I am the only one who can choose to give or withdraw my own love.

I also said a prayer for the woman. She may have been loud and abrasive, but at that point, she was probably just miserable. What she needed was not judgment from me, but a blessing of love and peace. I offered it to God right there in the dress section, and I don't know if it changed her at all, but I learned something about spirituality that day. It is more than something you read and talk about; it's only real when you live it.

I often wonder if our impatience with others' inabilities to live what we may already understand only mirrors the frustration we feel for ourselves, because we cannot truly live that concept either.

We *know* that we should love people, yet we may harshly judge someone whom we feel is unloving. Surely, our dichotomy rings some distant alarm in Heaven. It's easy to adore people who are easy to love, but to love the perpetrator? That is when the wheels of what we understand hit the pavement of how we actually live.

Our principles are not the problem. It is that we are impatient, if not a little condescending, with others who don't know as much as we do (or as much as we *think* we do). We make statements like, "They just don't get it," and we are happy to discuss that fact freely with others who do "get it."

Perhaps we are the ones who just don't get it. Yes, maybe we have broadened our understanding or gained a few inches on our spiritual quest, but we're never really going to "get it" until what we have to offer the world is love without reservation, condition, or judgment. Most likely, the frustration we feel with the unloving culprit is a reflection of our own pain because we can't love freely with or without a good reason—as if there really were such a thing.

Perhaps our knowledge of truth may have

positioned us one step closer to spiritual perfection, but that also makes us more accountable. Others may be fumbling in the dark with their actions, but when we are judgmental and unloving with all the lights of truth shining, surely we are the ones who have the most learning to do.

I have often wondered if other people on spiritual paths have encountered a similar predicament. In The Old Testament, Moses went up to mount Sinai and spent forty days with God receiving instructions and a set of stone tablets containing the law "written with the finger of God" (Exodus 31:18). When he came back to the people, he found that instead of worshipping the true God with whom he had just spent forty days, they had constructed a golden calf to adore instead. Angry at their behavior, he broke the stone tablets he had for them.

The Lord asked him to come up to the mountain again, and the next time he came down with what we now refer to as the Ten Commandments. A powerful prophet and leader, Moses' life emulated obedience. I am inclined to believe that he obeyed the commandments with exactness, such as keeping the Sabbath day holy and not coveting his neighbor's property.

There is one particular commandment that makes me wonder: *Love thy neighbor as thyself* (Leviticus 19:18). How did he do it? How did he open his heart to the people who so easily closed their own hearts to the God he personally knew and worshipped? How did he serve those who were willing to serve dumb idols rather than their own Creator? When Moses was on the mountain, He saw the Lord's finger engrave the commandment of love on the stone, and certainly, he believed in it. Nevertheless, I wonder if he spent those next many years in the wilderness struggling to love them—the same way we often struggle to love each other.

Like Moses, as seekers in this day, we should continue to climb our own peaks to spend time with God and learn His truths. Yet it will always be on the ground where we meld these principles into our character.

We must continue the never-ending quest to become connected to our Eternal Creator and to live by the awe-inspiring truths that will free us from bondage. However, as we progress on this path, we cannot use the knowledge we acquire to condemn those around us. We are bound simply to share it with them. When we freely love others and honor their unique paths, we are better able to serve as a guide. As we carry God's truth and His love with us, we draw closer to one of life's most transcendent principles—joy is most deeply experienced, when we are walking on the ceiling together.

Footnotes

[1] Tolle, Eckhart, *Stillness Speaks* (Novato, CA: New World Library, 2003), 1.

[2] Gibran, Kahlil, *The Broken Wings* (New York: NY: The Citadel Press, 1957), 48.

[3] Kabat-Zinn, John, *Wherever You Go There You Are* (New York, NY: Hyperion, 1994), 4.

[4] Thoreau, Henry David, *Walden* (New York, NY: Barnes and Noble Inc., 1993), 275.

[5] Cameron, Julia, *The Right to Write* (New York, NY: Penguin Putnam, 1998), xvi.

[6] Allen, James, *As a Man Thinketh* (New York, NY: Barnes and Noble, 1992), 20.

[7] Cornell, Ann Weiser, *The Power of Focusing* (New York, NY: Barnes and Noble, 1990), 16–17.

[8] Goleman, Daniel, *Emotional Intelligence* (New York, NY: Bantam Books, 1997), 47.

[9] Tolle, Eckhart, *The Power of Now* (Novato: CA: New World Library, 1999), 69.

[10] Bennett-Goleman, Tara, *Emotional Alchemy* (New York, NY: Three Rivers Press, 2001), 34.

[11] Ford, Debbie, *The Dark Side of the Light Chasers* (New York, NY: Riverhead Books, 1998), 72.

[12] Ibid, (121–122).

[13] Cameron, Julia, *Heart Steps* (New York, NY: Penguin Putnam, 1997), 3.

[14] Remen, Rachel Naomi, *My Grandfather's Blessing* (New York, NY: Riverhead Books, 2000), 218.

[15] Goodman, Ted, *The Forbes Book of Business Quotations* (New York, NY: Black Dog & Leventhal Publishers, Inc., 1997), 29.

[16] Spence, Gerry, *Give Me Liberty* (New York, NY: St. Martin's Griffin, 1998), 158–159.

[17] Deyer, Wayne, *Manifest Your Destiny* (New York, NY: Harper Collins, 1998), xiv.

[18] *The names of the individuals indicated here have been omitted from the text to preserve our friendship. But you know who you are . . .*

[19] Kabat-Zinn, John, *Wherever You Go There You Are* (New York, NY: Hyperion, 1994), 76.

Contact Heather Madder at
contact@HeatherMadder.com
or order more copies of this book at

TATE PUBLISHING, LLC

127 East Trade Center Terrace
Mustang, Oklahoma 73064

(888) 361 - 9473

TATE PUBLISHING, LLC
www.tatepublishing.com